SADLIER-OXFORD                    LEVEL A

# Vocabulary
# Workshop
## Enhanced Edition

The classic program for:

- *developing* and *enhancing* vocabulary resources

- *promoting* more effective communication in today's world

- *improving* vocabulary skills assessed on standardized and/or college-admission tests

By
**Jerome Shostak**

**Sadlier-Oxford**

A Division of William H. Sadlier, Inc.
9 Pine Street
New York, New York 10005-1002
1-800-221-5175

# Contents

Copyright © 1996 by
Sadlier-Oxford,
A Division of
William H. Sadlier, Inc.

ISBN: 0-8215-0606-4
10 11 12 13 / 04 03 02 01 00

Home Office: 9 Pine Street
New York, NY 10005-1002
1-800-221-5175

Requests for permission to make copies of any part of the work should be mailed to:

Permissions Department
William H. Sadlier, Inc.
9 Pine Street
New York, New York 10005-1002

# Foreword

For close to five decades VOCABULARY WORKSHOP has been a highly successful tool for guiding and stimulating systematic vocabulary growth for students. It has also been extremely valuable for preparing students to take the types of standardized vocabulary tests commonly used to assess grade placement, competence for graduation, and/or college readiness. The *Enhanced Edition* has faithfully maintained those features that have made the program so beneficial in these two areas, while introducing new elements to keep abreast of changing times and changing standardized-test procedures, particularly the SAT. The features that make VOCABULARY WORKSHOP so valuable include:

**Word List**
Each book contains 300 or more basic words, selected on the basis of:
- currency in present-day usage
- frequency on recognized vocabulary lists
- applicability to standardized tests
- current grade-placement research

**Units**
The words in each book are organized around 15 short, stimulating *Units* featuring:
- pronunciation and parts of speech
*New!* - definitions—fuller treatment in the *Enhanced Edition*
- synonyms and antonyms
- usage (one phrase and two sentences)

**Reviews**
Five *Reviews* highlight and reinforce the work of the units through challenging exercises involving:
*New!* - shades of meaning (SAT-type critical-thinking exercise)
- definitions
- synonyms and antonyms
- analogies
- sentence completions
- word families

**Cumulative Reviews**
Four *Cumulative Reviews* utilize standardized testing techniques to provide ongoing assessment of word mastery, all involving SAT-type critical-thinking skills. Here the exercises revolve around
*New!* - shades of meaning
- analogies
- two-word completions

**Additional Features**
- A *Diagnostic Test* provides ready assessment of student needs at the outset of the term.
- The *Vocabulary of Vocabulary* reviews terms and concepts needed for effective word study.
- The *Final Mastery Test* provides end-of-term assessment of student achievement.
- *Building with Word Roots* introduces the study of etymology.
- *Enhancing Your Vocabulary,* Levels F through H, introduces students to the study of word clusters.
*New!* - *Working with Parts of Speech,* Levels F through H, provides further work with word clusters and introduces 50 new words per level.

**Ancillary Materials**
- An *Answer Key* for each level supplies answers to all materials in the student text.
- A *Series Teacher's Guide* provides a thorough overview of the features in each level, along with tips for using them effectively.
- The *Supplementary Testing Program: Cycle One, Cycle Two* provide two complete programs of separate and different testing materials for each level, so testing can be varied. A *Combined Answer Key* for each level is also available.
- The SAT-type *TEST PREP Blackline Masters* for each level provide further testing materials designed to help students prepare for SAT-type standardized tests.
- An *Interactive Audio Pronunciation Program* is also available for each level.

# Pronunciation Key

The pronunciation is indicated for every basic word introduced in this book. The symbols used for this purpose, as listed below, are similar to those appearing in most standard dictionaries of recent vintage. The author has consulted a large number of dictionaries for this purpose but has relied primarily on *Webster's Third New International Dictionary* and *The Random House Dictionary of the English Language (Unabridged)*.

There are, of course, many English words for which two (or more) pronunciations are commonly accepted. In virtually all cases where such words occur in this book, the author has sought to make things easier for the student by giving just one pronunciation. The only significant exception occurs when the pronunciation changes in accordance with a shift in the part of speech. Thus we would indicate that *project* in the verb form is pronounced prə 'jekt, and in the noun form, 'präj ekt.

It is believed that these relatively simple pronunciation guides will be readily usable by the student. It should be emphasized, however, that the *best* way to learn the pronunciation of a word is to listen to and imitate an educated speaker.

## Vowels

| | | | | | |
|---|---|---|---|---|---|
| ā | lake | e | stress | ü | loot, new |
| a | mat | ī | knife | ů | foot, pull |
| â | care | i | sit | ə | rug, broken |
| ä | bark, bottle | ō | flow | ər | bird, better |
| aů | doubt | ô | all, cord | | |
| ē | beat, wordy | oi | oil | | |

## Consonants

| | | | | | |
|---|---|---|---|---|---|
| ch | child, lecture | s | cellar | wh | what |
| g | give | sh | shun | y | yearn |
| j | gentle, bridge | th | thank | z | is |
| ŋ | sing | t̶h̶ | those | zh | measure |

All other consonants are sounded as in the alphabet.

## Stress

The accent mark *precedes* the syllable receiving the major stress: en 'rich

## Parts of Speech

| | | | | | |
|---|---|---|---|---|---|
| *adj.* | adjective | *int.* | interjection | *prep.* | preposition |
| *adv.* | adverb | *n.* | noun | *v.* | verb |
| | | *part.* | participle | | |
| | | *pl.* | plural | | |

# The Vocabulary of Vocabulary

There is a large group of words in English that describe how words are used and how they are related to each other. We may call this the "vocabulary of vocabulary." Learning to understand and use terms of this type will help you to organize your study of words and to get better results in your vocabulary-building program.

Some of the terms in this group that you should know are given below. The exercises in each section will give you a chance to practice and to gain full mastery of the terms and the ideas they represent.

## Synonyms and Antonyms

**Synonyms**

A *synonym* is a word that has the same (or almost the same) meaning as another word.

EXAMPLES:

under—beneath        do—perform
final—last           pile—heap

**Exercises**

*In each of the following groups, encircle the word that is most nearly **the same** in meaning as the first word in **boldface type**.*

**1. silent**
a. noisy
b. kind
c. quiet
d. playful

**2. rule**
a. cover
b. leave
c. change
d. govern

**3. entire**
a. short
b. complete
c. worried
d. weary

**4. spring**
a. walk
b. ride
c. jump
d. drive

**5. rough**
a. easy
b. smooth
c. coarse
d. ready

**6. tidy**
a. neat
b. sloppy
c. poor
d. helpful

**7. section**
a. part
b. theater
c. stadium
d. whole

**8. craving**
a. feast
b. hunger
c. fullness
d. anger

**Antonyms**

An *antonym* is a word that is opposite (or almost opposite) in meaning to another word.

EXAMPLES:

hire—fire           crowded—empty
grief—joy           beneath—above

**Exercises**

*In each of the following groups, encircle the word that is most nearly **opposite** in meaning to the first word in **boldface type**.*

**1. fail**
a. lose
b. close
c. open
d. succeed

**2. create**
a. make
b. suggest
c. destroy
d. reveal

**3. depressed**
a. unhappy
b. possible
c. joyful
d. intelligent

**4. bend**
a. lengthen
b. straighten
c. frighten
d. tighten

2

| **5. guilt** | **6. definite** | **7. healthy** | **8. drowsy** |
|---|---|---|---|
| a. innocence | a. tardy | a. sturdy | a. alert |
| b. sentence | b. unusual | b. messy | b. quiet |
| c. freedom | c. vague | c. bossy | c. sleepy |
| d. judgment | d. certain | d. sickly | d. skinny |

## Words Pronounced Alike; Words Spelled Alike

**Homonyms**

A *homonym* is a word having the same (or almost the same) pronunciation as another word but a different meaning and a different spelling.

EXAMPLES:
piece—peace   be—bee
pane—pain   pair—pear

*Exercises*

*In each of the following sentences, encircle in the parentheses the* **homonym** *that correctly completes the meaning.*

1. I want (**some, sum**) of them for myself.
2. It is time for the (**flower, flour**) to bloom.
3. She hurt her (**heal, heel**) when she tripped.
4. He is the (**air, heir**) to a large fortune.
5. I don't care where you have (**bin, been, bean**)!
6. This is (**Ant, Aunt**) Edna, my father's youngest sister.
7. I could never shoot a (**deer, dear**), even for food!
8. When I grow up, I hope to (**sail, sale**) in my own ship.
9. I am positive that I have (**red, read**) that book.
10. Will you sew this (**seam, seem**) for me now?
11. We have gone (**through, threw**) that already!
12. The star of the rodeo was (**throne, thrown**) by the wild bronco.

**Homographs**

A *homograph* is a word having the same spelling as another word but a different meaning.

EXAMPLES:

*Cross* may mean *angry.*
Being contradicted always makes her *cross.*

*Cross* may mean *to pass or travel through.*
Please be careful when you *cross* the street.

*Cross* may mean *a pair of crossed lines.*
Place a *cross* at the spot where the accident occurred.

**Exercises**  In Column C, write the **homograph** suggested by the definitions given in Columns A and B. In each case, one word will fit both definitions. The first letter of each of the missing words is given in Column C. The dashes indicate the letters to be filled in.

| Column A | Column B | Column C |
|---|---|---|
| **1.** discharge | flames | f _ _ _ |
| **2.** remainder | sleep | r _ _ _ |
| **3.** large animal | carry | b _ _ _ |
| **4.** seashore | glide downhill | c _ _ _ _ |
| **5.** not heavy | not dark | l _ _ _ _ |
| **6.** cruel | intend | m _ _ _ |
| **7.** nation | say | s _ _ _ _ |
| **8.** touched | heavy cloth | f _ _ _ |
| **9.** place for a game | place of trial | c _ _ _ _ |
| **10.** part of a wheel | become weary | t _ _ _ |

## Parts of a Word

**Prefix**  A *prefix* is a syllable (or syllables) placed at the beginning of a word.

EXAMPLES:  de- ante- pro- ab-

**Suffix**  A *suffix* is a syllable (or syllables) placed at the end of a word.

EXAMPLES:  -ation -ancy -ed -ing

**Root**  A *root* or *base* is the main part of the word to which a prefix or a suffix may be added.

EXAMPLES:  -tain -fer- -ceive- -lief-

**Exercises**  Divide each of the following words into its prefix, root, and suffix. Some of the words may lack either a prefix, a suffix, or both. The first word has been done for you.

| Word | Prefix | Root | Suffix |
|---|---|---|---|
| **1. disturbance** | dis | turb | ance |
| **2. excitement** | | | |
| **3. reference** | | | |
| **4. chiefly** | | | |
| **5. receipt** | | | |
| **6. transferal** | | | |

# Denotation and Connotation

**Denotation**
The *denotation* of a word is its specific dictionary definition.

EXAMPLES:

| Word | Denotation |
|------|------------|
| peerless | without equal |
| lethal | deadly |
| specimen | a sample |

**Connotation**
The *connotation* of a word is its tone—that is, the emotions or associations it normally arouses in people using, hearing, or reading it. Depending on what these feelings are, the connotation of a word may be *favorable (positive)* or *unfavorable (pejorative)*. A word that does not normally arouse strong emotions of any kind has a *neutral* connotation.

EXAMPLES:

| Word | Connotation |
|------|-------------|
| peerless | favorable |
| lethal | unfavorable |
| specimen | neutral |

*Exercises*
*In the space provided, label the connotation of each of the following words* **F** *for "favorable,"* **U** *for "unfavorable," or* **N** *for "neutral."*

_____ **1.** fork     _____ **5.** quote     _____ **9.** gallant

_____ **2.** snobbish     _____ **6.** ruthless     _____ **10.** stingy

_____ **3.** gracious     _____ **7.** envious     _____ **11.** see

_____ **4.** sleep     _____ **8.** modesty     _____ **12.** cook

# Literal and Figurative Usage

**Literal Usage**
When a word or expression is being used in a *literal* sense, it is being employed in its strict (or primary) dictionary meaning in a situation (or *context*) that "makes sense" from a purely logical point of view.

EXAMPLE:
When we *cross that bridge,* we will be in New York.

**Figurative Usage**
Sometimes words or expressions are used in a symbolic or nonliteral way in situations that do not "make sense" from a purely logical point of view. We call this non-literal or "extended" application of a word or expression a *figurative* or *metaphorical* usage.

EXAMPLE:
"I realize that this decision may mean trouble for us down the road," said the Senator, "but we'll *cross that bridge* when we come to it."

**Exercises**   In the space provided, write **L** for "literal" or **F** for "figurative" next to each of the following sentences to show how the italicized expression is being used.

_____ **1.** When I was a boy, one of my favorite dishes was the savory hunter's *stew* that Grandmother used to make.

_____ **2.** When our luggage failed to appear at the airport baggage terminal, we really began to *stew.*

_____ **3.** The shortstop *fielded* the sharp grounder and threw out the runner at the plate.

_____ **4.** The new press secretary *fielded* the reporters' questions like a seasoned pro.

# Analogies

An analogy is a comparison. For example, we can make an analogy, or comparison, between a computer and the human brain.

In examinations you may be asked to find the relationship between two words. Then to show that you understand the relationship, you are asked to choose another pair of words that show the same relationship.

EXAMPLE:   **close** is to **open** as
a. dance is to swim
b. talk is to discuss
c. imprison is to release
d. hold is to grasp

Note that *close* and *open* are opposite in meaning. Of the four choices given, which pair is made up of words that are also opposite in meaning? The answer, clearly, is *c, imprison is to release.*

**Exercises**   In each of the following, encircle the item that best completes the analogy.

**1. fox** is to **clever** as
a. chicken is to brave
b. snake is to honest
c. owl is to foolish
d. mule is to stubborn

**2. groan** is to **pain** as
a. laugh is to sorrow
b. yawn is to weariness
c. wink is to fear
d. frown is to happiness

**3. penny** is to **dime** as
a. nickel is to quarter
b. dime is to dollar
c. quarter is to penny
d. dime is to half-dollar

**4. page** is to **book** as
a. baseball is to football
b. leaf is to tree
c. cover is to magazine
d. letter is to note

**5. mean** is to **kindness** as
a. brave is to courage
b. faithful is to loyalty
c. foolish is to wisdom
d. sincere is to honesty

**6. bright** is to **dull** as
a. courteous is to polite
b. dark is to cloudy
c. tidy is to neat
d. close is to distant

# Context Clues

When you do the various word-omission exercises in this book, look for *context clues* built right into the passage to guide you to the correct answer.

**Restatement Clues**

A *restatement clue* consists of a synonym for, or a definition of, a missing word.

EXAMPLE:

The noise and commotion in the crowded gymnasium were so great that we could barely make ourselves heard above the _____ .
a. score     b. referees     (c.) din     d. bleachers

**Contrast Clues**

A *contrast clue* consists of an antonym for, or a phrase meaning the opposite of, a missing word.

EXAMPLE:

When bad weather prevented the bomber from striking the (**(primary,)** **secret**) target, the pilot guided the plane to the secondary objective.

**Situational Clues**

The *situation* outlined in the sentence suggests the sense of the word that is wanted but does not state the meaning directly.

EXAMPLE:

Those in the audience who agreed with the speaker _____ their _____ by cheering, while those who disagreed booed.

a. registered . . . boredom     c. indicated . . . horror
(b.) expressed . . . approval     d. showed . . . dislike

---

*Exercises*   *Use context clues to choose the word or words that best complete each of the following sentences.*

**1.** The climbers inched their way to the top of the peak until at last they stood

upon the very _____ of the mountain.

a. bottom          b. slope          c. range          d. summit

**2.** There were a few moments of excitement in the first set, but on the whole it was an extremely (**thrilling, monotonous**) tennis match.

**3.** After we measured out the _____ that the recipe called for,

we used a mixer to _____ them in a bowl.

a. amounts . . . separate          c. ingredients . . . combine
b. directions . . . shred          d. temperature . . . bake

# Diagnostic Test

This Diagnostic Test contains a sampling of the words that are presented in this Vocabulary Workshop. It will give you an idea of the types and levels of the words to be studied. When you have gone through all the units, the Final Mastery Test will measure your ability to understand and use the words. By comparing your results on the Final Mastery Test with those on the Diagnostic Test below, you will have a basis for judging your progress.

*In each of the following groups, encircle the item that best expresses the meaning of the word in* **boldface type** *in the introductory phrase.*

**1. mimic** my way of speaking
a. notice        b. study            c. improve        d. imitate

**2. forsake** their comrades
a. call together   b. desert          c. protect        d. arm

**3. an ingenious** scheme
a. clever        b. wicked          c. clumsy         d. childish

**4. designate** her successor
a. dislike       b. name            c. criticize      d. fire

**5. a self-seeking** attitude
a. selfish       b. noble           c. intelligent    d. effective

**6. rummaged** in the attic
a. hid           b. cleaned up      c. searched       d. played

**7. a strapping** fellow
a. timid         b. husky           c. hardworking    d. dependable

**8.** as his troubles **receded**
a. grew worse    b. remained        c. retreated      d. grew larger

**9.** broke his **vow**
a. sword         b. arm             c. habit          d. promise

**10.** having **global** significance
a. little        b. unexpected      c. worldwide      d. personal

**11. sage** advice
a. wise          b. odd             c. old-fashioned  d. foolish

**12.** share our **reveries**
a. profits       b. dreams          c. troubles       d. possessions

**13. topple** the government
a. join          b. strengthen      c. threaten       d. overthrow

**14.** an **acute** attack
a. unpleasant    b. fatal           c. severe         d. mild

**15.** a **gory** horror movie
a. successful    b. bloody          c. new            d. long

**16. a synopsis** of the play
a. performance    b. review    c. summary    d. defense

**17. pacify** the angry customers
a. arrest    b. calm    c. scold    d. ignore

**18. vie** for the championship
a. compete    b. travel    c. rehearse    d. cheat

**19. dissect** the report
a. accept    b. reject    c. make fun of    d. analyze

**20. a pathetic** sight
a. vivid    b. humorous    c. moving    d. unexplained

**21. quash** a rebellion
a. lead    b. crush    c. explain    d. start

**22. blighted** the neighborhood
a. beautified    b. rebuilt    c. lived in    d. ruined

**23.** traffic **fatalities**
a. lights    b. expenditures    c. regulations    d. deaths

**24.** an **inflammatory** speech
a. fiery    b. boring    c. long-winded    d. informal

**25.** the **plight** of the homeless
a. misfortune    b. wealth    c. hopes    d. hard work

**26.** took **optional** courses
a. easy    b. advanced    c. not required    d. difficult

**27. taut** nerves
a. strong    b. tense    c. weak    d. damaged

**28.** show remarkable **discretion**
a. judgment    b. courage    c. pride    d. carelessness

**29. verging on** insanity
a. helping to cure    b. coming close to    c. preventing    d. far removed from

**30.** plan to **rendezvous** at a certain place
a. eat    b. meet    c. dance    d. sleep

**31.** an **unerring** aim
a. noble    b. uncertain    c. unfailing    d. hurried

**32. foil** the plot
a. cover up    b. defeat    c. join    d. help

**33.** made **rigorous** demands
a. expected    b. tough    c. fair    d. easy

**34.** an **extinct** animal
a. vanished    b. tame    c. common    d. local

**35.** a useful **implement**
a. person    b. idea    c. animal    d. tool

**36. enumerate** the rules
a. list    b. enforce    c. break    d. change

**37.** a **far-fetched** excuse
a. convincing      b. unlikely          c. written            d. overused

**00.** show **scant** concern
a. great           b. false             c. very little        d. sincere

**39.** the **indisputable** leader
a. unquestioned    b. powerful          c. experienced        d. cruel

**40.** **abduct** the official
a. introduce       b. kidnap            c. fire               d. elect

**41.** **adhere to** his promise
a. break           b. explain           c. stick to           d. listen to

**42.** **disquieting** news
a. upsetting       b. sensational       c. funny              d. encouraging

**43.** with a **serene** expression on her face
a. worried         b. cruel             c. peaceful           d. surprised

**44.** built a **replica** of the ship
a. side            b. copy              c. deck               d. mast

**45.** **amalgamated** their forces
a. disbanded       b. weakened          c. led                d. combined

**46.** **confiscated** the weapon
a. sold            b. seized            c. hid                d. displayed

**47.** a **wholesome** development
a. bad             b. popular           c. healthy            d. strange

**48.** stored the **data** in the computer
a. surplus         b. information       c. supplies           d. equipment

**49.** a **sluggish** economy
a. competitive     b. slow-moving       c. free               d. growing

**50.** **relish** the idea
a. hate            b. ignore            c. delight in         d. examine

# Unit 1

**Definitions**

*Note carefully the spelling, pronunciation, and definition of each of the following words. Then write the word in the illustrative phrase following*

1. **apparel**
(ə 'par əl)

(*n.*) clothing, that which serves as dress or decoration; (*v.*) to put clothes on, dress up

suitable _____ for the occasion

2. **besiege**
(bi 'sēj)

(*v.*) to attack by surrounding with military forces; to cause worry or trouble

_____ the enemy city

3. **compress**
(*v.*, kəm 'pres; *n.*, 'käm pres)

(*v.*) to press together; to reduce in size or volume; (*n.*) a folded cloth or pad applied to an injury

a cold _____

4. **denounce**
(di 'naúns)

(*v.*) to condemn openly; to accuse formally

_____ the tyrant's crimes

5. **dispatch**
(dis 'pach)

(*v.*) to send off or out for a purpose; to kill; (*n.*) an official message; promptness, speed; the act of killing

_____ a messenger

6. **douse**
(daús)

(*v.*) to plunge into a liquid, drench; to put out quickly, extinguish

_____ the flames

7. **expressly**
(ek 'spres lē)

(*adv.*) plainly, in so many words; for a particular purpose

_____ stated his approval

8. **famished**
('fam isht)

(*adj., part.*) suffering severely from hunger or from lack of something

_____ for news of home

9. **forsake**
(fôr 'sāk)

(*v.*) to give up, renounce; to leave, abandon

_____ one's friends

10. **gainful**
('gān fəl)

(*adj.*) profitable; bringing in money or some special advantage

work that is more enjoyable than _____

11. **immense**
(i 'mens)

(*adj.*) very large or great; beyond ordinary means of measurement

_____ natural resources

12. **inept**
(in 'ept)

(*adj.*) totally without skill or appropriateness

_____ at dealing with people

13. **ingenious**
(in 'jēn yəs)

(*adj.*) showing remarkable originality, inventiveness, or resourcefulness; clever

an _____ solution to the problem

**14. instantaneous**
(in stən 'tā nē əs)

(*adj.*) done in an instant; immediate

gave us an _____ response

**15. irk**
(ərk)

(*v.*) to annoy, trouble, make weary

_____ by numerous foolish questions

**16. libel**
('lī bəl)

(*n.*) a statement that unfairly or falsely harms the reputation of the person about whom it is made; (*v.*) to write or publish such a statement

find guilty of _____

**17. misgiving**
(mis 'giv iŋ)

(*n.*) a feeling of fear, doubt, or uncertainty

had _____ about joining that club

**18. oaf**
(ōf)

(*n.*) a stupid person; a big, clumsy, slow individual

a lazy _____

**19. recede**
(ri 'sēd)

(*v.*) to go or move backward; to become more distant

as the floodwaters _____

**20. repast**
(ri 'past)

(*n.*) a meal, food

enjoy a light _____

---

**Completing the Sentence**

*Choose the word from this unit that best completes each of the following sentences. Write it in the space given.*

1. Since it was well past their lunchtime by the time we arrived home, the children were _____ .

2. The laws of this land do not shield public figures from just criticism, but they do protect them against _____ .

3. The terms of our agreement _____ forbade us to take any of the goods for our own use.

4. Far away on the horizon, we saw the tiny figures of a lonely traveler and his mule _____ into the sunset.

5. A(n) _____ will be sent to all our representatives in Latin America advising them how to handle the problem.

6. Because I have reached an age at which I am unwilling to depend on my parents, I am out to find _____ employment.

7. Some of life's rewards are _____ ; others are a long time in coming.

8. When you are really hungry, even the simplest foods will be a delicious _____ .

**9.** While all true vegetarians _____ animal meats, some do eat dairy products.

**10.** None of us could figure out how the _____ magician had managed to escape from the trunk submerged in the tank of water.

**11.** Some people hailed the man as a genius; others _____ him as a quack.

**12.** As an inexperienced sailor, I had more than a few _____ about taking out the small boat in such rough weather.

**13.** Don't allow yourself to be _____ by every small trouble that may arise during the day.

**14.** How can we hope to _____ a city that is surrounded by such strong walls and has ample supplies of everything it needs?

**15.** When you try to play tennis for the first time, you are going to find that your attempts to hit the ball are very _____ .

**16.** If you _____ all the items as much as possible, you will be able to get everything into a single suitcase.

**17.** Let's make certain to _____ the fire before leaving camp.

**18.** She had no right to call me a clumsy _____ just because I spilled some water on her.

**19.** Your _____ can be neat and attractive without being expensive.

**20.** On my first baby-sitting job, I found that one must have _____ patience to take care of small children.

---

**Synonyms**   *Choose the word from this unit that is most nearly **the same** in meaning as each of the following groups of expressions. Write the word on the line given.*

**1.** a meal; food, victuals   _____

**2.** to bother, annoy, irritate, vex   _____

**3.** clumsy, unskilled, bungling, incompetent   _____

**4.** a slander, slur; to smear, bad-mouth   _____

**5.** vast, enormous, immeasurable, gigantic   _____

**6.** imaginative, inventive, resourceful, clever   _____

**7.** a bonehead, dunce; a clod, lout   _____

**8.** clothing, attire, garments; to deck out   _____

**9.** to retreat, go back, back up, ebb   _____

**10.** a doubt, worry, qualm, hesitation

**11.** condemn, criticize, censure

**12.** clearly, pointedly, explicitly

**13.** to slay; a report, communication

**14.** to desert, abandon, give up, disown

**15.** to submerge, soak, dunk, immerse

**16.** to condense, shrink, shorten

**17.** hungry, starving, ravenous

**18.** prompt, quick, speedy

**19.** moneymaking, paying, profitable

**20.** to blockade, encircle; to pressure, hound

---

**Antonyms**      *Choose the word from this unit that is most nearly*
***opposite*** *in meaning to each of the following groups of*
*expressions. Write the word on the line given.*

**1.** to advance, come closer

**2.** to keep, hold on to, stand by

**3.** unimaginative, unoriginal, uninventive

**4.** well fed, full, satisfied, satiated

**5.** skillful, accomplished, adroit

**6.** delayed, slow, gradual

**7.** small, tiny, minute, infinitesimal

**8.** a feeling of confidence, assurance

**9.** to dry out, dehydrate; to kindle, ignite

**10.** unprofitable, unrewarding, nonpaying

**11.** to expand, enlarge

**12.** to please, delight, cheer, gladden

**13.** to undress, unclothe, strip, denude

**14.** to recall, to withhold

**15.** to hail, acclaim

**16.** implicitly; accidentally

14

**Choosing the Right Word**   *Encircle the **boldface** word that more satisfactorily completes each of the following sentences.*

1. His conceit is so (**immense, gainful**) that he cannot imagine anyone voting against him in the election for class president.

2. Her conscience forced her to (**denounce, libel**) the conspirators to the authorities.

3. When I realized that I was thoroughly prepared for the final exams, my fears quickly (**receded, irked**).

4. He may claim that we have (**libeled, dispatched**) him, but we have facts to back up every statement made in the column about him.

5. Which job would you take—one that is more (**inept, gainful**) right now or one that pays a small salary but offers a chance for valuable training?

6. Where did he ever get the curious idea that we set up this volleyball court (**expressly, instantaneously**) for him and his friends?

7. Tom may not be as polished and clever as some of the other boys, but I think it is unfair of you to call him a(n) (**dispatch, oaf**).

8. (**Famished, Compressed**) for a chance to see her work in print, the young writer begged the magazine editor to publish her story.

9. I always feel sad in the autumn, when the trees lose their beautiful (**repast, apparel**) of leaves.

10. You may criticize the roads and the lights, but the fact is that most car accidents are caused by (**inept, immense**) drivers.

11. As soon as she took over the office of Mayor, she was (**besieged, dispatched**) by dozens of people eager to get city jobs.

12. Instead of feeling (**libeled, irked**) because you did poorly on the exam, why don't you make up your mind to study harder?

13. Each day, after she finishes her homework, she enjoys a light (**repast, misgiving**) of the detective stories she loves so well.

14. As soon as he began his long, boring speech, our excitement died down, as though we had been (**receded, doused**) with cold water.

15. After all the bad things he has done, I feel no (**dispatches, misgivings**) about telling him that I don't want him to be my "friend" anymore.

16. We were pleasantly surprised to see that she completed the difficult task we had given her with neatness and (**irk, dispatch**).

17. We can (**compress, besiege**) the message of the sermon into one short sentence: "Do unto others as you would have others do unto you."

18. I will never (**recede, forsake**) the people who helped me in my hour of need!

19. We are working hard to improve conditions in our community, but we cannot expect (**gainful, instantaneous**) results.

20. His notebooks show that Leonardo da Vinci was not only a masterful artist but an (**inept, ingenious**) inventor as well.

# Unit 2

**Definitions** *Note carefully the spelling, pronunciation, and definition of each of the following words. Then write the word in the illustrative phrase following*

**1. adverse**
(ad 'vərs)

(*adj.*) unfavorable, negative; working against, hostile

an _____ reaction

**2. arid**
('ar id)

(*adj.*) extremely dry; uninteresting, dull

a region too _____ for farming

**3. assailant**
(ə 'sā lənt)

(*n.*) a person who attacks violently (with blows or words)

injured by an unknown _____

**4. billow**
('bil ō)

(*n.*) a large wave; (*v.*) to rise or swell like a wave

sailing over the _____

**5. confront**
(kən 'frənt)

(*v.*) to meet face-to-face, especially as a challenge

want to _____ my accusers

**6. constrain**
(kən 'strān)

(*v.*) to force, compel; to restrain, hold back

feel _____ to follow orders

**7. contemporary**
(kən 'tem pə rer ē)

(*adj.*) belonging to the same period of time as oneself; (*n.*) a person of the same time

prefers to associate with her _____

**8. depict**
(di 'pikt)

(*v.*) to portray; to represent or show in the form of a picture

_____ the scene on canvas

**9. disinterested**
(dis 'in trəst id)

(*adj.*) fair-minded, free from selfish motives; indifferent

a _____ judge

**10. encompass**
(en 'kəm pəs)

(*v.*) to encircle, go or reach around; to enclose; to include with a certain group or class

the oceans that _____ the world

**11. groundless**
('graùnd ləs)

(*adj.*) without any good reason or cause, unjustified

_____ fears

**12. hypocrite**
('hip ə krit)

(*n.*) a person who pretends to be what he or she is not or better than he or she really is

an artful _____

**13. incomprehensible**
(in käm pri 'hen sə bəl)

(*adj.*) impossible to understand

found the explanation _____

**14. manipulate**
(mə 'nip yə lāt)

(*v.*) to handle or use skillfully; to manage or control for personal gain or advantage

able to _____ tools well

**15. maximum**
('mak sə məm)

(*n.*) the greatest possible amount or degree; (*adj.*) reaching the greatest possible amount or degree

a _____ _____ strength tablet

**16. mimic**
('mim ik)

(*n.*) a person who does imitations; (*v.*) to imitate; to make fun of

_____ my way of talking

**17. ruffle**
('rəf əl)

(*v.*) to wrinkle, make uneven; to annoy, upset; to flip through; (*n.*) a gathered strip of material used for trimming edges; a ripple; a low drumbeat

_____ my feelings

**18. serene**
(sə 'rēn)

(*adj.*) peaceful, calm; free of emotional upset; clear and free of storm; majestic, grand

_____ in the face of trouble

**19. sheepish**
('shēp ish)

(*adj.*) embarrassed; resembling a sheep in meekness, timid

with a _____ grin on his face

**20. stamina**
('stam ə nə)

(*n.*) the strength needed to keep going or overcome physical or mental strain, endurance

the _____ of a long-distance runner

---

**Completing the Sentence**

*Choose the word from this unit that best completes each of the following sentences. Write it in the space given.*

1. This basic textbook _____ all the information you will have to master for the entrance examination.

2. The _____ expression on her face showed that she was totally undisturbed by the confusion and turmoil around her.

3. A breeze sprang up and began to _____ the smooth and tranquil surface of the water.

4. Since Tom is both smart and _____ , I think he is just the person to decide which of us is right in this long and bitter quarrel.

5. Held back by _____ winds, the plane arrived at the airport two hours late.

6. Fortunately, I was able to fight off my _____ , even though his attack took me by complete surprise.

7. Parrots and a few other kinds of birds can _____ sounds, particularly human speech.

8. As you become a more skillful driver, you will be able to _____ all the controls of the car while keeping your eyes on the road.

**2**

**9.** For a long time, I thought that he was a good and sincere person, but I finally saw that he was no more than a(n) _____.

**10.** You and Lucy will never settle your quarrel unless you _____ each other directly and listen to what the other person has to say.

**11.** I was so embarrassed by my blunder that I could do nothing but grin in a(n) _____ and self-conscious way.

**12.** The jury found the defendant "not guilty" because they were convinced that the charges against her were _____ .

**13.** Using the entire east wall of the new Post Office building, the painter tried to _____ the founding of our city.

**14.** The hot, _____ climate of Arizona is favorable for many people suffering from various diseases, such as arthritis.

**15.** Although I may hurt your feelings, my conscience _____ me to tell you exactly what is on my mind.

**16.** You talk so fast and in such a low tone of voice that you are going to be completely _____ to most people.

**17.** Under the law, the _____ number of people who may ride in this bus is seventy-five.

**18.** The brisk breeze caused the sheets on the line to _____ like the sails on a yacht that is running with the wind.

**19.** The skyscraper is one of the best-known forms of _____ architecture.

**20.** Very few starting pitchers have the _____ to pitch well for nine innings.

---

**Synonyms**  *Choose the word from this unit that is most nearly **the same** in meaning as each of the following groups of expressions. Write the word on the line given.*

**1.** endurance, staying power  _____

**2.** greatest, largest, highest; utmost  _____

**3.** waterless, parched; boring, unimaginative  _____

**4.** to handle, work, maneuver; exploit  _____

**5.** to imitate, parrot; a copycat  _____

**6.** embarrassed, shamefaced; timid, meek  _____

**7.** baffling, confusing, bewildering  _____

**8.** unfavorable; difficult, trying  _____

18

**9.** a two-faced person, phony _____

**10.** tranquil, composed; fair; august _____

**11.** to compel, pressure; to restrict _____

**12.** present-day, modern, current _____

**13.** neutral, impartial, unbiased; apathetic _____

**14.** to face, encounter, come to grips with _____

**15.** a wave, breaker; to swell, surge _____

**16.** to upset, annoy; a frill _____

**17.** baseless, unsupported, unjustified _____

**18.** an assaulter, attacker, mugger _____

**19.** to sketch, draw, picture, represent _____

**20.** to surround, envelop; to include, comprise _____

**Antonyms**   *Choose the word from this unit that is most nearly **opposite** in meaning to each of the following groups of expressions. Write the word on the line given.*

**1.** to leave out, omit, exclude _____

**2.** to smooth out, to soothe _____

**3.** partial, biased, prejudiced _____

**4.** well watered; waterlogged, soggy; fertile, lush _____

**5.** ancient, prehistoric, antique _____

**6.** least, lowest, minimum, smallest _____

**7.** a victim, prey, injured party _____

**8.** well-founded, reasonable, justified _____

**9.** understandable, clear, plain, intelligible _____

**10.** favorable, positive, helpful, beneficial _____

**11.** a trough; to deflate, collapse _____

**12.** to avoid, evade, sidestep _____

**13.** agitated, troubled; stormy, inclement _____

**14.** bold, saucy, brazen, confident _____

**15.** to loosen, liberate, unfetter, relax _____

**Choosing the Right Word**  *Encircle the **boldface** word that more satisfactorily completes each of the following sentences.*

1. Instead of working so hard to (**mimic, encompass**) the popular TV stars, why don't you try to develop an acting style of your own?

2. After many stormy years in the service of his country, George Washington retired to the (**serene, adverse**) life of his beloved Mount Vernon.

3. I didn't want to (**ruffle, manipulate**) the feelings of the hotel manager, but I felt that I had to complain about the miserable service.

4. The (**adverse, sheepish**) publicity that he received during the investigation was probably the cause of his defeat in the next election.

5. Despite the fact that she was in shock, the victim gave a clear description of her (**hypocrite, assailant**).

6. A good scientist must have a keen mind, an unquenchable curiosity, and a(n) (**groundless, disinterested**) desire to discover the truth.

7. The big-league shortstop (**manipulates, constrains**) his glove like a magician, snaring every ball hit within reach.

8. Martin Luther King, Jr., and Robert F. Kennedy were (**contemporaries, mimics**) born within a few years of each other.

9. The science program in our school (**depicts, encompasses**) biology, chemistry, physics, earth science, and other related sources.

10. My idea of a (**mimic, hypocrite**) is a person who gives advice that he or she is not willing to follow.

11. After living for many years in that roomy old farmhouse, I felt awfully (**adverse, constrained**) in that small apartment.

12. Anyone who has ever sailed a small boat knows how thrilling it is to feel the spray in your face while the sails (**billow, encompass**) overhead.

13. After giving a few (**sheepish, disinterested**) excuses, the two swimmers packed up and left the private beach.

14. We expected the lecture on the energy crisis to be exciting, but it turned out to be an (**adverse, arid**) rundown of well-known facts and figures.

15. What a relief to learn that my parents had been delayed by a storm, and that all my fears about an accident were (**groundless, serene**)!

16. If you (**billow, confront**) your problems honestly and openly, instead of trying to hide them, you will have a better chance of solving them.

17. She has many interesting ideas, but she seems to lack the physical and mental (**stamina, assailant**) to make good use of them.

18. Do you think it would be a good idea to set a (**maximum, contemporary**) figure for the amount of homework any teacher is allowed to assign?

19. Her decision not to accept our sincere offer of assistance is completely (**disinterested, incomprehensible**) to me.

20. She has gained success as a writer who knows how to (**confront, depict**) in a lifelike way the hopes, fears, and problems of young people today.

# Unit 3

*Note carefully the spelling, pronunciation, and definition of each of the following words. Then write the word in the illustrative phrase following.*

**1. barrage**
(bə 'räzh)

(*n.*) a rapid, large-scale outpouring of something

a _____ of questions

**2. bigot**
('big ət)

(*n.*) an intolerant, prejudiced person

a narrow-minded _____

**3. designate**
('dez ig nāt)

(*v.*) to indicate, point out; to appoint; (*adj.*) selected but not yet installed

will _____ the scholarship winners

**4. diversity**
(di 'vər sə tē)

(*n.*) difference, variety; a condition of having many different types or forms

a person with a _____ of interests

**5. enigma**
(i 'nig mə)

(*n.*) someone or something that is extremely puzzling; that which cannot be understood or explained

found the movie's plot an _____

**6. gloat**
(glōt)

(*v.*) to look at or think about with great intensity and satisfaction; to take great personal joy in

_____ over one's success

**7. global**
('glō bəl)

(*adj.*) of, relating to, or involving the entire world; comprehensive

a _____ communications system

**8. illusion**
(i 'lü zhən)

(*n.*) a false idea; something that one seems to see or to be aware of that really does not exist

an optical _____

**9. infuriate**
(in 'fyùr ē āt)

(*v.*) to make very angry, enrage

_____ one's parents

**10. motivate**
('mō tə vāt)

(*v.*) to provide with a reason for doing; to push on to some goal or course of action

_____ the students to work harder

**11. pacifist**
('pas ə fist)

(*n.*) one who is against war or the use of violence; (*adj.*) opposing war or violence

_____ protesting the war

**12. queue**
(kyü)

(*n.*) a line of people waiting for something (such as a bus or the opening of a store); (*v.*) to form such a line

a long _____ at the bus stop

**13. restrict**
(ri 'strikt)

(*v.*) to keep within set limits; to confine or limit

_____ one's intake of food

**14. sage**
(sāj)

(*adj.*) wise; (*n.*) a very wise person

_____ advice

**15. slake**
(slāk)

(*v.*) to satisfy, relieve, or bring to an end

_____ one's thirst

**16. terrain**
(tə 'rān)

(*n.*) the landscape, especially considered with regard to its physical features or fitness for some use; a field of knowledge

rugged _____

**17. vocation**
(vō 'kā shən)

(*n.*) any trade, profession, or occupation; a sense of fitness or special calling for one's work

found my true _____

**18. vow**
(vau̇)

(*n.*) a solemn or sacred promise or pledge; (*v.*) to declare or promise in a solemn way

make a _____ of eternal devotion

**19. waylay**
('wā lā)

(*v.*) to lie in wait for and attack, ambush

_____ the stragglers

**20. wither**
('with ər)

(*v.*) to dry up, wilt, sag; to cause someone to feel ashamed, humiliated, or very small

hands _____ with age

---

**Completing the Sentence**

*Choose the word from this unit that best completes each of the following sentences. Write it in the space given.*

**1.** The rich _____ of plant and animal life in a tropical rain forest never ceases to amaze me.

**2.** The police now believe that the mugger _____ the elderly woman as she entered the elevator of her apartment house.

**3.** For better or for worse, as you become older and more experienced, you will lose many of the comforting _____ of youth.

**4.** The deadly _____ of shells from our guns pinned down the enemy troops on the narrow beach where they had landed.

**5.** No decent person will _____ over someone else's failures or misfortunes.

**6.** Since he greatly enjoys woodworking, and also makes a living from it, his hobby and his _____ are one and the same.

**7.** Because the show is scheduled to end after midnight, the management will _____ admission to people over sixteen.

**8.** How sad it is to see such beautiful flowers _____ and die!

**9.** Is it possible to be a(n) _____ in a world where so many people are using force to take unfair advantage of others?

**10.** The pollution problem, far from being limited to the United States, is truly _____ in scope.

**11.** The desire to be the world's top tennis player _____ the young woman to spend hours every day improving her game.

**12.** As she was sworn in, she made a(n) _____ that she would never use the powers of her office for selfish or unworthy purposes.

**13.** The animals in the drought area traveled for many miles to reach a body of water where they could _____ their thirst.

**14.** I don't understand what he is aiming at or why he behaves as he does; in fact, his whole personality is a(n) _____ to me.

**15.** Nothing _____ my boss more than an employee who is late for work and then offers a foolish excuse for not arriving on time.

**16.** Our hike was not very long, but the _____ was so rocky and hilly that we were exhausted by the time we reached our goal.

**17.** A person can usually tell how popular a new movie is by the length of the _____ out in front of the box office.

**18.** Even before the new President took office, he _____ the men and women who were to serve in his cabinet.

**19.** Like a typical _____ , he believes that any customs different from his own are "wrong" and "uncivilized."

**20.** I came to regard my grandmother as a(n) _____ whose wisdom helped to solve many family problems.

---

**Synonyms**      *Choose the word from this unit that is most nearly **the same** in meaning as each of the following groups of expressions. Write the word on the line given.*

**1.** to shrivel, wilt, droop; to shame, abash      _____

**2.** variety, dissimilarity, difference      _____

**3.** to quench, gratify, sate; to ease, assuage      _____

**4.** to ambush, attack, entrap, ensnare      _____

**5.** to relish, revel in; to crow over      _____

**6.** a philosopher, Solomon; wise, sagacious      _____

**7.** a pledge, word of honor; to pledge      _____

**8.** someone who is prejudiced or biased      _____

**9.** a delusion, fantasy, deception  _____

**10.** worldwide, universal; widespread  _____

**11.** someone who is against war or violence  _____

**12.** to provoke, incense, madden, enrage  _____

**13.** a profession, career, trade, pursuit  _____

**14.** a bombardment, shelling, volley, blast  _____

**15.** to spur on, encourage, prompt, goad  _____

**16.** ground, topography; territory  _____

**17.** to signify, denote; to nominate, choose  _____

**18.** a riddle, mystery, puzzle, conundrum  _____

**19.** a column, file, row, line  _____

**20.** to hold back, limit, confine  _____

---

**Antonyms**   *Choose the word from this unit that is most nearly* **opposite** *in meaning to each of the following groups of expressions. Write the word on the line given.*

**1.** local, regional, provincial  _____

**2.** similarity, sameness, uniformity  _____

**3.** to bloom, flower, flourish, burgeon  _____

**4.** a fool, dunce; foolish, unwise  _____

**5.** to open up, enlarge, expand  _____

**6.** to calm, soothe, pacify, please  _____

**7.** to discourage, dissuade, disincline  _____

**8.** a warmonger, saber-rattler  _____

**9.** to regret, bemoan, mourn, feel chagrined  _____

**10.** a milling and disorganized crowd  _____

**11.** reality, truth, actuality  _____

**12.** to increase, intensify, aggravate  _____

**13.** a hobby, pastime, avocation  _____

**14.** someone without prejudice  _____

**15.** someone you can "read" like an open book  _____

24

*Encircle the **boldface** word that more satisfactorily completes each of the following sentences.*

1. The applicants for the job will have to (**queue, slake**) up in an orderly way and wait their turns to be interviewed.

2. With the other team 10 points ahead and only a few minutes left to play, our hopes of victory began to (**wither, gloat**).

3. When the speaker asked for opinions from the audience, he was greeted with a (**barrage, terrain**) of critical remarks and angry questions.

4. To (**slake, designate**) our curiosity, you will have to tell us everything that happened during that strange trip.

5. Has it ever occurred to you that your belief that you are a superior person and a natural leader may be no more than a(n) (**illusion, vocation**)?

6. As the defense attorney left the courtroom, he was (**waylaid, withered**) by a group of eager reporters trying to get a statement from him.

7. A good loser doesn't sulk over defeat; a good winner doesn't (**gloat, vow**) over victory.

8. The United States has laws that (**restrict, waylay**) the numbers and kinds of immigrants allowed to enter this country.

9. By the time you are ready to enter the workforce, many (**vocations, bigots**) that are important today may not even exist anymore.

10. World War II was a truly (**global, pacifist**) struggle, fought in all parts of the world by people of every race and background.

11. Since you have so many prejudices of your own, you should think twice before you accuse other people of being (**pacifists, bigots**).

12. Just how and why two people fall in love is a(n) (**queue, enigma**) that no scientist has ever been able to explain.

13. A great teacher not only makes the material of the course understandable but also (**designates, motivates**) the students to want to learn more.

14. No matter what it may cost me to carry out, I will never break my sacred (**vow, illusion**).

15. She is never bored because she has a great (**enigma, diversity**) of interests, ranging from folk dancing to mathematics.

16. Before we begin our backpacking trip, we should have a good idea of the (**terrain, vocation**) we are going to cover.

17. Entangled in the trapper's net, the (**infuriated, withered**) lion roared in helpless fury.

18. The children who are admitted free to the ball game will be allowed to sit only in certain (**designated, motivated**) parts of the stands.

19. Her analysis of what is wrong with our city government seems to me remarkably (**sage, global**) and helpful.

20. Since I am convinced that violence always creates more problems than it solves, I have become a (**pacifist, bigot**).

# Review Units 1–3

**Analogies**  *In each of the following, encircle the item that best completes the comparison.*

1. **enigma** is to **puzzlement** as
   a. illusion is to satisfaction
   b. vow is to horror
   c. libel is to pleasure
   d. misgiving is to uncertainty

2. **marathon** is to **stamina** as
   a. award is to money
   b. election is to manipulation
   c. sprint is to speed
   d. prize is to strength

3. **sage** is to **wisdom** as
   a. assailant is to skill
   b. bigot is to prejudice
   c. pacifist is to fear
   d. mimic is to wealth

4. **global** is to **world** as
   a. cosmic is to universe
   b. lunar is to sun
   c. aquatic is to star
   d. colonial is to planet

5. **inept** is to **skill** as
   a. serene is to calmness
   b. immense is to size
   c. ignorant is to knowledge
   d. ingenious is to cleverness

6. **jacket** is to **apparel** as
   a. chair is to furniture
   b. ruffle is to equipment
   c. horse is to utensil
   d. rope is to machine

7. **famished** is to **eat** as
   a. sleepy is to write
   b. fatigued is to wear
   c. exhausted is to play
   d. thirsty is to drink

8. **hypocrite** is to **insincere** as
   a. fool is to sage
   b. oaf is to clumsy
   c. assailant is to sheepish
   d. dunce is to ingenious

9. **thirst** is to **slake** as
   a. fire is to extinguish
   b. city is to besiege
   c. family is to forsake
   d. pest is to irk

10. **desert** is to **arid** as
    a. plateau is to flat
    b. valley is to high
    c. stream is to broad
    d. mountain is to low

11. **sheepish** is to **embarrassment** as
    a. delighted is to disgust
    b. infuriated is to anger
    c. puzzled is to contentment
    d. bored is to enthusiasm

12. **hand** is to **manipulate** as
    a. foot is to denounce
    b. head is to compress
    c. nose is to designate
    d. eye is to observe

13. **pacifist** is to **war** as
    a. glutton is to food
    b. vegetarian is to meat
    c. drunkard is to liquor
    d. piper is to smoking

14. **invisible** is to **see** as
    a. inaccurate is to correct
    b. incomprehensible is to understand
    c. inclined is to do
    d. intelligent is to know

15. **douse** is to **liquid** as
    a. kindle is to flame
    b. dispatch is to air
    c. freeze is to heat
    d. thaw is to snow

16. **nosh** is to **repast** as
    a. blizzard is to tornado
    b. thunderstorm is to breeze
    c. flood is to heat wave
    d. shower is to hurricane

17. **inventor** is to **ingenious** as
    a. showoff is to sheepish
    b. judge is to disinterested
    c. child is to incomprehensible
    d. champion is to inept

18. **big** is to **immense** as
    a. high is to wide
    b. black is to green
    c. small is to tiny
    d. smooth is to rough

**19. painter** is to **depict** as
a. dancer is to compose
b. sculptor is to suggest
c. author is to hide
d. mimic is to imitate

**20. gainful** is to **profit** as
a. groundless is to substance
b. informative is to knowledge
c. penniless is to money
d. uniform is to diversity

**Definitions**    *In each of the following, encircle the word that is best defined or suggested by the introductory expression.*

**1.** a heavy outpouring (as of questions)
a. barrage        b. queue          c. compress       d. serene

**2.** a person whose prejudices are always showing
a. pacifist       b. oaf            c. bigot          d. mimic

**3.** a person's lifework or career
a. terrain        b. libel          c. stamina        d. vocation

**4.** an idea not based on reality
a. irk            b. waylay         c. illusion       d. sage

**5.** a solemn promise
a. vow            b. repast         c. apparel        d. douse

**6.** to provoke anger
a. billow         b. infuriate      c. recede         d. ruffle

**7.** living at the same time
a. gainful        b. maximum        c. global         d. contemporary

**8.** having no substance or foundation
a. ingenious      b. disinterested  c. groundless     d. sheepish

**9.** one who pretends to be better than he or she really is
a. hypocrite      b. assailant      c. besiege        d. wither

**10.** a feeling of doubt or uneasiness
a. confront       b. diversity      c. misgiving      d. incomprehensible

**11.** to include or enclose within certain boundaries
a. depict         b. encompass      c. manipulate     d. denounce

**12.** to provide a reason or purpose for doing something
a. motivate       b. restrict       c. forsake        d. designate

**13.** to quench
a. slake          b. constrain      c. gloat          d. dispatch

**14.** totally lacking skill or appropriateness
a. instantaneous  b. inept          c. immense        d. arid

**15.** something that is deeply puzzling
a. adverse        b. expressly      c. famished       d. enigma

**16.** to hold someone back
a. constrain      b. vow            c. wither         d. slake

**17.** calm and composed
a. sheepish       b. gainful        c. instantaneous  d. serene

**Shades of Meaning**   *Read each sentence carefully. Then encircle the item that best completes the statement below the sentence.*

The well-dressed gentleman of the late eighteenth century wore ruffles of sheer linen or lace at his throat and wrists.   **(2)**

**1.** In line 1 the word **ruffles** most nearly means
a. wrinkles
b. gathered trimmings
c. ripples
d. irritations

In computer terminology a global command is one that applies to an entire file, document, or program.   **(2)**

**2.** The word **global** in line 1 is best defined as
a. worldwide
b. widespread
c. random
d. comprehensive

When compresses failed to slow the bleeding, medics applied a tourniquet above the soldier's wound.   **(2)**

**3.** The word **compresses** in line 1 is used to mean
a. bandage pads
b. medicines
c. condensations
d. reductions

In keeping with his strong pacifist beliefs, the poet Robert Lowell served a prison term for refusing to bear arms during World War II.   **(2)**

**4.** In line 1 the word **pacifist** most nearly means
a. militant
b. criminal
c. old-fashioned
d. antiwar

Before they are confirmed by the Senate, those whom the President selects for cabinet posts are termed "secretaries designate."   **(2)**

**5.** The word **designate** in line 2 is used to mean
a. veteran
b. resigned
c. nominated
d. experienced

---

**Antonyms**   *In each of the following groups, encircle the word or expression that is most nearly **opposite** in meaning to the word in **boldface type** in the introductory phrase.*

**1. expressly** planned for us
a. purposely
b. by accident
c. quickly
d. cleverly

**2.** felt **famished**
a. frozen
b. confident
c. overfed
d. hungry

**3.** an **adverse** reaction
a. fatal
b. harmful
c. positive
d. puzzling

**4.** a **disinterested** observer
a. wise
b. prejudiced
c. bored
d. foreign

**5.** an **arid** plot of land
a. soggy
b. large
c. expensive
d. distant

**6. infuriate** a customer
a. anger
b. cheat
c. delight
d. ignore

**7.** gave us a **sheepish** look
a. unfriendly     b. bold     c. timid     d. silly

**8.** of **global** significance
a. local     b. worldwide     c. vast     d. unmeasured

**9.** keeps student interest at a **maximum**
a. low point     b. high point     c. distance     d. boiling point

**10.** found him **incomprehensible**
a. puzzling     b. understandable     c. interesting     d. boring

**11.** will not **forsake** my friends
a. help     b. stand by     c. hire     d. leave

**12.** has **immense** powers
a. illegal     b. vast     c. useless     d. small

**13.** a person's **vocation**
a. job     b. house     c. family     d. hobby

**14.** **sage** advice
a. foolish     b. wise     c. strange     d. unexpected

**15.** a **contemporary** writer
a. intelligent     b. puzzling     c. ancient     d. famous

---

**Completing the Sentence**     *From the following lists of words, choose the one that best completes each of the sentences below. Write the word in the space provided.*

### Group A

| | | | |
|---|---|---|---|
| **gloat** | **dispatch** | **besiege** | **bigot** |
| **confront** | **mimic** | **inept** | **compress** |

**1.** She was so _____ with calls from well-wishers that she found it hard to get away to eat breakfast.

**2.** How can I _____ a lifetime of experience into a five-minute talk?

**3.** The Mayor decided to _____ extra police units to the scene of the rioting.

**4.** I intend to _____ him as soon as possible and demand an explanation of his unfair remarks.

**5.** I think it is very bad taste on your part to _____ a person with a speech defect.

### Group B

| | | | |
|---|---|---|---|
| **depict** | **designate** | **queue** | **apparel** |
| **douse** | **stamina** | **serene** | **encompass** |

**1.** Because our players lacked _____ , they tired quickly in the second half and lost the game.

2. Instead of milling around in front of the ticket window, why don't you form a(n) _____ and get your tickets in an orderly way?

3. It is up to our English teacher to _____ the students who will enter the essay-writing contest.

4. We carefully _____ our campfire before we left the picnic grounds.

5. How can I hope to _____ in mere words the depths of despair to which I have sunk?

---

## Word Families

**A.** *On the line provided, write a **noun form** of each of the following words.*

EXAMPLE: compress — **compression**

1. denounce _____
2. recede _____
3. confront _____
4. besiege _____
5. depict _____
6. encompass _____
7. manipulate _____
8. designate _____
9. infuriate _____
10. motivate _____
11. immense _____
12. restrict _____
13. ingenious _____
14. adverse _____
15. arid _____

**B.** *On the line provided, write an **adjective** related to each of the following.*

EXAMPLE: vocation — **vocational**

1. oaf _____
2. hypocrite _____
3. enigma _____
4. libel _____
5. diversity _____
6. illusion _____

**C.** *On the line provided, write a* **verb** *related to each of the following words.*

EXAMPLE: gainful — **gain**

1. maximum _____
2. diversity _____
3. assailant _____
4. incomprehensible _____
5. pacifist _____

---

**Filling the Blanks**  *Encircle the pair of words that best complete each of the following passages.*

1. The demand for tickets to the play-offs was so heavy that for days the box office was _____ like some embattled fortress by mobs of people waiting more or less impatiently in long _____ that snaked endlessly around the whole block.

   a. denounced . . . enigmas
   b. besieged . . . queues
   c. confronted . . . ruffles
   d. encompassed . . . billows

2. It took a great deal of _____ to keep up with the rest of the pack as they sped across the broken and hilly _____ that separated them from the finish line in the cross-country race.

   a. dispatch . . . apparel
   b. misgiving . . . repast
   c. stamina . . . terrain
   d. diversity . . . barrage

3. As the travelers crossed the hot and _____ wasteland known as the Sahara Desert, their eyes were deceived more than once by mirages and other optical _____ .

   a. adverse . . . mimics
   b. immense . . . vocations
   c. groundless . . . enigmas
   d. arid . . . illusions

4. Two ruffians _____ the weary traveler on a lonely stretch of road, but the man was able to beat off his _____ with the help of his stout staff.

   a. waylaid . . . assailants
   b. dispatched . . . oafs
   c. confronted . . . hypocrites
   d. constrained . . . pacifists

5. Though other people have been moved to action by high ideals, Thomas Alva Edison, one of the most _____ inventors ever to be produced by this country, seems in part to have been _____ simply by the love of a challenge.

   a. disinterested . . . manipulated
   b. ingenious . . . motivated
   c. inept . . . infuriated
   d. immense . . . dispatched

# Unit 4

**Definitions** — *Note carefully the spelling, pronunciation, and definition of each of the following words. Then write the word in the illustrative phrase following.*

**1. acquit**
(ə 'kwit)

(*v.*) to declare not guilty, free from blame, discharge completely; to conduct or behave (oneself)

_____ them of the charge

**2. deem**
(dēm)

(*v.*) to think, believe; to consider, have an opinion

_____ it a wise step

**3. devastate**
('dev ə stāt)

(*v.*) to destroy, lay waste

_____ the countryside

**4. discredit**
(dis 'kred it)

(*v.*) to throw doubt upon, cause to be distrusted; to damage in reputation; (*n.*) a loss or lack of belief, confidence, or reputation

_____ the witness's story

**5. elusive**
(ē 'lü siv)

(*adj.*) difficult to catch or to hold; hard to explain or understand

an _____ halfback

**6. generate**
('jen ə rāt)

(*v.*) to bring into existence; to be the cause of

_____ electricity

**7. idolize**
('ī dəl īz)

(*v.*) to worship as an idol, make an idol of; to love very much

_____ the movie star

**8. ingratitude**
(in 'grat ə tüd)

(*n.*) a lack of thankfulness

hurt by such _____

**9. keepsake**
('kēp sāk)

(*n.*) something kept in memory of the giver; a souvenir

gave me a locket as a _____

**10. mortal**
('môr tel)

(*n.*) a being that must eventually die; (*adj.*) of or relating to such a being; causing death, fatal; possible, conceivable

a _____ wound

**11. ovation**
(ō 'vā shən)

(*n.*) an enthusiastic public welcome, an outburst of applause

receive a standing _____

**12. petty**
('pet ē)

(*adj.*) unimportant, trivial; narrow-minded; secondary in rank, minor

_____ criticisms

**13. plight**
(plīt)

(*n.*) a condition or state (usually bad); (*v.*) to pledge, promise solemnly

the _____ of the homeless

**14. repent**
(ri ′pent)

(v.) to feel sorry for what one has done or has failed to do

_____ _____ the mistakes of my youth

**15. reverie**
(′rev ə rē)

(n.) a daydream; the condition of being lost in thought

in a deep _____

**16. revocation**
(rev ə ′kā shən)

(n.) an act or instance of calling back, repealing; an annulment, cancellation

the _____ of an agreement

**17. scan**
(skan)

(v.) to examine closely; to look over quickly but thoroughly; to analyze the rhythm of a poem; (n.) an examination

_____ the horizon

**18. strand**
(strand)

(n.) a beach or shore; a string of wire, hair, etc.; (v.) to drive or run aground; to leave in a hopeless position

_____ the base runners

**19. strife**
(strīf)

(n.) bitter disagreement; fighting, struggle

a veteran of political _____

**20. topple**
(′täp əl)

(v.) to fall forward; to overturn, bring about the downfall of

_____ from the shelf

---

**Completing the Sentence**

*Choose the word from this unit that best completes each of the following sentences. Write it in the space given.*

**1.** The defendant was warned that another speeding ticket would result in the _____ of her driver's license.

**2.** Though that actress's name and face are all but forgotten today, she used to be _____ by adoring fans all over the world.

**3.** Suddenly the racket produced by a noisy car radio rudely awakened me from my peaceful _____ .

**4.** The TV program made us keenly aware of the _____ of elderly people trying to live on Social Security payments.

**5.** The famous "Leaning Tower of Pisa" looks as though it were going to _____ over any minute.

**6.** The rope is made of many _____ of fiber woven together.

**7.** The hurricane so _____ a large section of the coast that the President declared it a disaster area.

**8.** We learned that even unfavorable reviews of a new book may help to _____ a certain amount of public interest in it.

**9.** The evidence against the accused man proved to be so weak that the jury had no choice but to _____ _____ him.

**10.** Since it is clear that his only interest is to make money for himself, his plan for building a new highway has been completely _____ .

**11.** Regardless of what you may think proper, I do not _____ it necessary for someone of your age to wear an evening gown to the dance.

**12.** I don't have the time to read every word of that long newspaper article, but I'll _____ it quickly to get the main idea.

**13.** Because the members of my family disagree on so many matters, the dinner table is often the scene of much verbal _____ .

**14.** I plan to save this old notebook as a(n) _____ of one of the best and most enjoyable classes I have ever had.

**15.** She richly deserved the _____ she received from the audience for her brilliant performance.

**16.** Why argue about such _____ matters when there are so many important problems to deal with?

**17.** Tom is not a very fast runner, but he is so _____ that he is extremely hard to tackle on the football field.

**18.** Since I sincerely appreciate all my parents have done for me, how can you accuse me of _____ ?

**19.** The wound at first did not appear to be too serious, but to our great grief it proved to be _____ .

**20.** Instead of telling us how much you _____ your outrageous conduct, why don't you sincerely try to reform?

---

**Synonyms**     *Choose the word from this unit that is most nearly **the same** in meaning as each of the following groups of expressions. Write the word on the line given.*

**1.** to worship, adore, revere                    _____

**2.** to overturn, unseat, upset, tumble          _____

**3.** a repeal, cancellation, withdrawal          _____

**4.** insignificant, minor, piddling              _____

**5.** a sorry state of affairs; to pledge         _____

**6.** conflict, struggle, discord, turmoil        _____

**7.** to abandon, maroon; a fiber, thread         _____

**8.** to regret, feel sorry for                   _____

**9.** to wreck, destroy, leave in ruins, desolate _____

**10.** cheers, bravos, hurrahs _____

**11.** to study; to glance at, skim; a survey _____

**12.** a daydream, fantasy, meditation _____

**13.** thanklessness, ungratefulness _____

**14.** to throw doubt on, disparage _____

**15.** to create, produce, beget; cause _____

**16.** slippery, wily; puzzling, baffling _____

**17.** a human; fleeting; fatal, extreme _____

**18.** to think, judge; to consider, regard _____

**19.** a souvenir, reminder, memento _____

**20.** to clear of blame, exonerate; dismiss _____

---

**Antonyms**     *Choose the word from this unit that is most nearly **opposite** in meaning to each of the following groups of expressions. Write the word on the line given.*

**1.** thankfulness, gratefulness, recognition _____

**2.** undying, everlasting, eternal; divine; a god _____

**3.** to confirm, corroborate, bolster _____

**4.** easy to catch, hold, or understand _____

**5.** to convict, declare guilty _____

**6.** to remain upright; to establish, set up _____

**7.** peace, calm, harmony, agreement _____

**8.** to have no regrets, rejoice over _____

**9.** to despise, scorn, disdain, detest _____

**10.** important, major, significant, weighty _____

**11.** to develop, improve _____

**12.** booing, jeering, the cold shoulder _____

**13.** a ratification, confirmation _____

**14.** to end, terminate, extinguish, stifle _____

**15.** to rescue, save, come to the aid of _____

**Choosing the Right Word**   *Encircle the **boldface** word that more satisfactorily completes each of the following sentences.*

1. What an (**ovation, reverie**) he received when he trotted back to the bench after scoring the winning touchdown!

2. I knew that she was wrapped up in herself, but I never dreamed that even she could be guilty of such (**discredit, ingratitude**).

3. Father often says that he has never stopped (**repenting, devastating**) the decision he made many years ago to give up the study of medicine.

4. While the actors were busy rehearsing, the manager ran away with all the money and left them (**stranded, plighted**) in a strange town.

5. Our business is barely managing to pay its bills; one bad break will be enough to (**acquit, topple**) it into bankruptcy.

6. Imagine his (**plight, ovation**) — penniless, unemployed, and with a large family to support!

7. By reelecting him to Congress, the court of public opinion has forever (**generated, acquitted**) him of the charges of neglecting his duties.

8. Many diseases that have disappeared in the United States continue to (**devastate, idolize**) countries in other parts of the world.

9. Once order had been restored, the leaders of the opposition called for the (**revocation, plight**) of martial law.

10. After so many years of (**strife, strand**) — in business, politics, and the family — he wants only to retire to the peace and quiet of his ranch.

11. We will never allow vicious rumors to (**deem, generate**) racial hatred in our school!

12. At times we all enjoy a(n) (**ovation, reverie**) about "what might have been," but before long we must return to "the way things are."

13. Our supervisor (**topples, scans**) the newspaper each morning for items that may serve as leads for the sales force.

14. At times it is quite natural to feel afraid, and it is certainly no (**discredit, keepsake**) to anyone to admit it.

15. In Shakespeare's *A Midsummer Night's Dream*, who is the character who speaks the line, "Lord, what fools these (**mortals, keepsakes**) be"?

16. Since you are the only one of us who has had experience with this kind of problem, we shall do whatever you (**deem, discredit**) necessary.

17. In my composition, I tried to give a definition of "humor," but I found the idea too (**petty, elusive**) to pin down.

18. A special edition of poems by the noted writer was presented as a (**keepsake, strand**) to all who attended her 80th birthday party.

19. We should respect our national leaders, but we should not (**idolize, discredit**) them and assume that they can do no wrong.

20. Are we going to allow (**mortal, petty**) quarrels to destroy a friendship that has been built up for so many years?

# Unit 5

**Definitions**

*Note carefully the spelling, pronunciation, and definition of each of the following words. Then write the word in the illustrative phrase following*

**1. acute**
(ə 'kyüt)

(*adj.*) with a sharp point; keen and alert; sharp and severe; rising quickly to a high point and lasting for a short time

a very _____ observer

**2. bluster**
('bləs tər)

(*v.*) to talk or act in a noisy and threatening way; to blow in stormy gusts; (*n.*) speech that is loud and threatening

not frightened by all your _____

**3. bungle**
('bəŋ gəl)

(*v.*) to act or work clumsily and awkwardly; to ruin something through clumsiness

_____ the job

**4. commentary**
('käm ən ter ē)

(*n.*) a series of notes clarifying or explaining something; an expression of opinion

a learned _____ on the Bible

**5. duration**
(dü 'rā shən)

(*n.*) the length of time that something continues or lasts

for the _____ of the storm

**6. eerie**
('ē rē)

(*adj.*) causing fear because of strangeness; weird, mysterious

an _____ ghost story

**7. facet**
('fas ət)

(*n.*) one aspect or side of a subject or problem; one of the cut surfaces of a gem

an important _____ of the problem

**8. fidelity**
(fi 'del ə tē)

(*n.*) the state of being faithful; accuracy in details, exactness

a high-_____ record

**9. fray**
(frā)

(*n.*) a brawl, noisy quarrel; (*v.*) to wear away by rubbing; make ragged or worn; to strain, irritate

_____ our nerves

**10. headstrong**
('hed strôŋ)

(*adj.*) willful, stubborn

a _____ child

**11. inhabitant**
(in 'hab ə tənt)

(*n.*) a person or animal living permanently in a given place

a lifelong _____ of this town

**12. numb**
(nəm)

(*adj.*) having lost power of feeling or movement; (*v.*) to dull the feelings of; to cause to lose feeling

cold that leaves the fingers _____

**13. pacify**
('pas ə fī)

(*v.*) to make peaceful or calm; to soothe

_____ the angry mob

**14. ravenous**
('rav ə nəs)

(*adj.*) greedy; very hungry; eager for satisfaction

a _____ appetite

**15. refute**
(ri 'fyüt)

(*v.*) to prove incorrect

_____ the statement

**16. remorse**
(ri 'mors)

(*n.*) deep and painful regret for one's past misdeeds

overcome with _____

**17. setback**
('set bak)

(*n.*) something that interferes with progress; a disappointment, unexpected loss or defeat; a steplike recession in a wall

suffered a severe _____

**18. smug**
(sməg)

(*adj.*) overly self-satisfied, self-righteous

an air of _____ superiority

**19. synopsis**
(si 'näp sis)

(*n.*) a brief statement giving a general view of some subject, book, etc.; a summary

read a _____ of the plot

**20. tarry**
('tar ē)

(*v.*) to delay leaving; to linger, wait; to remain or stay for a while

tempted to _____ longer

---

**Completing the Sentence**

*Choose the word from this unit that best completes each of the following sentences. Write it in the space given.*

1. Our team suffered a tough _____ when our best player was hurt in the first few minutes of play.

2. After the dentist gave me an injection of novocaine, the whole side of my jaw turned _____ .

3. Warmth and understanding are two of the outstanding _____ of her personality.

4. Because of our inexperience and haste, we _____ the little repair job so badly that it became necessary to replace the entire motor.

5. Although the rain was heavy, it was of such short _____ that it didn't interfere with our plans.

6. The program contained a(n) _____ of the opera, so that we were able to follow the action even though the singing was in Italian.

7. I had a(n) _____ feeling that we were being followed and that something bad might happen.

**8.** Because I _____ at the book fair, I was ten minutes late for my piano lesson.

**9.** No one can question her complete _____ to basic American ideas and ideals.

**10.** Some children are as docile as sheep; others are as _____ as mules.

**11.** After eating a light breakfast and hiking for hours in the crisp mountain air, you can imagine how _____ we were by lunchtime.

**12.** The accused person must be given every chance to _____ the charges against him or her.

**13.** When my two sisters began their bitter quarrel, only Mother had enough nerve to enter the _____ and tell them to stop.

**14.** Anyone who has never had a sprained ankle will find it hard to imagine how _____ the pain is.

**15.** By _____ in a loud, confident voice, he tried to convince us that he had nothing to do with the accident.

**16.** Do you think it is a good idea to try to _____ the weeping child by giving her a lollipop?

**17.** His _____ expression showed how highly he valued his own opinions and scorned the views of others.

**18.** The newscaster on my favorite TV program not only tells the facts of the news but offers a(n) _____ that helps us to understand it.

**19.** Since the convicted felon had shown no _____ for his crimes, the judge sentenced him to the maximum prison term allowed.

**20.** Is it true that the _____ of Maine are sometimes called "Mainiacs"?

---

**Synonyms**     *Choose the word from this unit that is most nearly **the same** in meaning as each of the following groups of expressions. Write the word on the line given.*

**1.** a side, aspect, element; a cut         _____

**2.** unfeeling, insensible; dazed; to deaden         _____

**3.** starved, famished; voracious, wolfish         _____

**4.** a failure, reversal; a defeat         _____

**5.** loyalty, faithfulness         _____

**6.** to remain, stay; to linger, dawdle, dally         _____

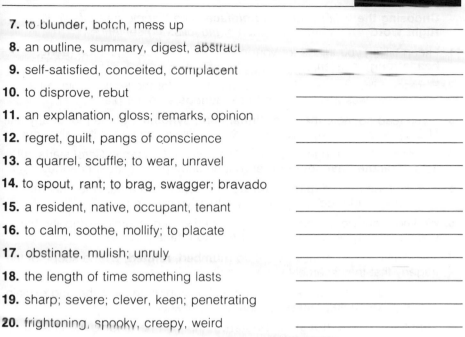

7. to blunder, botch, mess up

8. an outline, summary, digest, abstract

9. self-satisfied, conceited, complacent

10. to disprove, rebut

11. an explanation, gloss; remarks, opinion

12. regret, guilt, pangs of conscience

13. a quarrel, scuffle; to wear, unravel

14. to spout, rant; to brag, swagger; bravado

15. a resident, native, occupant, tenant

16. to calm, soothe, mollify; to placate

17. obstinate, mulish; unruly

18. the length of time something lasts

19. sharp; severe; clever, keen; penetrating

20. frightening, spooky, creepy, weird

---

**Antonyms**    Choose the word from this unit that is most nearly *opposite* in meaning to each of the following groups of expressions. Write the word on the line given.

1. not hungry; well-fed, satisfied, satiated

2. obedient, docile, submissive

3. undisturbing, untroubling

4. sensitive, having feeling; alert

5. to rush, hasten; to leave, depart

6. to prove, support, confirm, corroborate

7. an advance, gain, progress; a triumph

8. a stranger, outsider, visitor, foreigner

9. a clear conscience, guiltlessness

10. dull, blunted; mild; stupid, obtuse

11. to anger, arouse; to stir up, foment, ignite

12. to accomplish skillfully

13. disloyalty, treachery; inexactness

14. discontented, disgruntled

40

**Choosing the Right Word**  *Encircle the **boldface** word that more satisfactorily completes each of the following sentences.*

1. I keep telling you things for your own good, but you're just too (**eerie, headstrong**) to listen.

2. Florence's illness, after she had been chosen for the leading role in the class show, was a serious (**setback, synopsis**) to our plans.

3. If you read no more than a(n) (**inhabitant, synopsis**) of the plot of any one of Shakespeare's plays, you will get very little idea of what it is all about.

4. The character Scrooge in Charles Dickens's *A Christmas Carol* starts out as a(n) (**acute, ravenous**) miser, but he undergoes a great change.

5. "It's your job to help (**pacify, refute**) the conquered area," the general said, "not to add fuel to an already explosive situation."

6. We know that we are going through a period of economic instability, but there is no way of telling what its (**duration, facet**) will be.

7. The victims of the disaster were so (**numbed, refuted**) by the scope of the tragedy that they scarcely showed any emotion at all.

8. The strength of this book lies in the author's ability to describe and explain different (**setbacks, facets**) of human experience.

9. After the way you (**bungled, blustered**) the job of arranging the class trip, I can never again trust you with anything important.

10. On the camping trip out West some of the children were frightened when they first heard the (**smug, eerie**) howls of coyotes at night.

11. The idea that most people usually behave in a calm and reasonable way is (**refuted, bungled**) by all the facts of history.

12. Each time she answered a question correctly, she rewarded herself with a (**smug, ravenous**) little smile of self-congratulation.

13. Although I don't agree with all her ideas, I must admire her unshakable (**fidelity, synopsis**) to them.

14. Since it had seemed that winter would (**tarry, pacify**) forever, we were all heartily glad when it finally quit dragging its heels and departed.

15. We cannot assume that all the people that one sees on the streets of a large city are actually (**facets, inhabitants**) of the place.

16. The fact that so many people are still living in poverty is indeed a sad (**fidelity, commentary**) on our civilization.

17. With a winter storm (**blustering, bungling**) outside, what could be more welcome than a warm room, a good meal, and my favorite TV program?

18. There is so much wear and tear on the ropes in this pulley system that they become (**frayed, refuted**) in only a few days.

19. His (**ravenous, acute**) analysis of the housing problem in our town gave us a clear idea of what we would have to overcome.

20. When I realized how deeply I had hurt my friend with my careless insult, I suffered a pang of (**remorse, bluster**).

# Unit 6

**Definitions**

*Note carefully the spelling, pronunciation, and definition of each of the following words. Then write the word in the illustrative phrase following.*

**1. agenda**
(ə 'jen də)

(*n.*) the program for a meeting, a list, outline, or plan of things to be considered or done

on today's _____

**2. amiable**
('ā mē ə bəl)

(*adj.*) friendly, good-natured

an _____ companion

**3. befuddle**
(bi 'fəd əl)

(*v.*) to confuse, make stupid

_____ me with so many details

**4. blight**
(blīt)

(*n.*) a disease that causes plants to wither and die; a condition of disease or ruin; (*v.*) to destroy, ruin

crops suffering from _____

**5. boisterous**
('boi strəs)

(*adj.*) rough and noisy in a cheerful way; high-spirited

a _____ crowd

**6. clarity**
('klar ə tē)

(*n.*) clearness, accuracy

explained with perfect _____

**7. compliant**
(kəm 'plī ənt)

(*adj.*) willing to do what someone else wants; obedient

too _____ to say no

**8. conserve**
(kən 'sərv)

(*v.*) to preserve; to keep from being damaged, lost, or wasted; to save

_____ our natural resources

**9. debut**
('dā byü)

(*n.*) a first public appearance; a formal entrance into society; (*v.*) to make a first appearance

made her _____ as a soloist

**10. gory**
('gôr ē)

(*adj.*) very bloody; marked by bloodshed, slaughter, or violence

a _____ battle

**11. gross**
(grōs)

(*adj.*) overweight; coarse, vulgar; very noticeable; total; (*n.*) an overall total (without deductions); twelve dozen; (*v.*) to earn

a _____ error in judgment

**12. induce**
(in 'düs)

(*v.*) to cause, bring about; to persuade

_____ sleep

**13. leeway**
('lē wā)

(*n.*) extra space for moving along a certain route; allowance for mistakes or inaccuracies; margin of error

allow yourself some _____

**...ber**
(..m bər)

(adj.) flexible; (v.) to cause to become flexible

_____ up before the race

**15. maze**
(māz)

(n.) a network of paths through which it is hard to find one's way; something very mixed-up and confusing

a _____ of back streets and alleys

**16. oracle**
('ôr ə kəl)

(n.) someone or something that can predict the future

a famous Greek _____

**17. partisan**
('pärt ə zən)

(n.) a strong supporter of a person, party, or cause; one whose support is unreasoning; a resistance fighter, guerrilla; (adj.) strongly supporting one side only

the _____ hometown fans

**18. reimburse**
(rē im 'bərs)

(v.) to pay back; to give payment for

_____ me for my expenses

**19. vacate**
('vā kāt)

(v.) to go away from, leave empty; to make empty; to void, annul

_____ the apartment

**20. vagabond**
('vag ə bänd)

(n.) an idle wanderer; a tramp; (adj.) wandering, unsettled; irresponsible

tramps and other _____

---

**Completing the Sentence**

*Choose the word from this unit that best completes each of the following sentences. Write it in the space given.*

**1.** If the Superintendent of Schools should _____ her position by resigning, the Mayor has the right to name someone else to the job.

**2.** We cannot allow the lives of millions of people to be _____ by poverty.

**3.** Before the game starts, the players _____ up by doing a few deep knee bends, sit-ups, and other exercises.

**4.** The high point of the social season was the formal _____ of young ladies at the annual Society Ball.

**5.** The high standard of excellence that the woman had set for herself left her no _____ for mistakes.

**6.** None of us could possibly overlook the _____ error that the waiter had made in adding up our check.

**7.** I was not prepared for the _____ sight that met my eyes at the scene of that horrible massacre.

**8.** Each of the items on the _____ for our meeting today will probably require a good deal of discussion.

**9.** Why do you ask me what's going to happen? I'm no _____ !

**10.** If you would be kind enough to buy a loose loaf notebook for me while you are in the stationery store, I'll _____ you immediately.

**11.** How can a mind _____ by alcohol make the type of snap decision needed to drive safely in heavy traffic?

**12.** Because our energy resources are limited, the American people must try to do everything possible to _____ fuel.

**13.** The crowd is so _____ that the umpire is booed every time he makes a decision against the home team.

**14.** Because of her outgoing and _____ personality, she is liked by everyone.

**15.** Trying to untangle a badly snarled fishing line is like trying to find one's way through a(n) _____ .

**16.** For years, his restless spirit led him to wander the highways and byways of this great land like any other footloose _____ .

**17.** No matter what you may say, you cannot _____ me to do something that I know is wrong

**18.** Mr. Fillmer explained with such _____ how to go about changing a tire that I felt that even someone as clumsy as I could do it.

**19.** You certainly have a right to cheer for your team, but try not to become too _____ and unruly.

**20.** Because you are working with older and more experienced people, you should be _____ with their requests and advice.

---

**Synonyms**   *Choose the word from this unit that is most nearly **the same** in meaning as each of the following groups of expressions. Write the word on the line given.*

**1.** flexible, supple, pliable; to stretch   _____

**2.** total; sheer, utter; flagrant; fat   _____

**3.** to cause, bring on; to persuade   _____

**4.** to confuse, bewilder, boggle, stupefy   _____

**5.** an eyesore; to spoil, ruin, nip   _____

**6.** bloody, gruesome   _____

**7.** a supporter, fan, booster; partial, biased   _____

**8.** a prophet, seer, sibyl   _____

**9.** a network, labyrinth, puzzle, tangle

**10.** latitude, allowance, elbowroom

**11.** to leave, depart; to give up, abandon

**12.** meek, docile, obedient, submissive

**13.** to repay, pay back, refund, compensate

**14.** to save, preserve, guard, care for

**15.** pleasant, agreeable, good-natured

**16.** noisy, loud, unruly, disorderly

**17.** clearness, lucidity, precision

**18.** a wanderer, vagrant, hobo; footloose

**19.** a list, schedule, docket

**20.** a first appearance, coming-out

---

**Antonyms**  Choose the word from this unit that is most nearly **opposite** in meaning to each of the following groups of expressions. Write the word on the line given.

**1.** confusion, murkiness, ambiguity

**2.** to occupy, keep, hold, hang on to

**3.** disobedient, obstinate, rebellious, perverse

**4.** quiet, calm, peaceful, well-behaved, sedate

**5.** to waste, squander, dissipate

**6.** a critic, foe; impartial, neutral

**7.** a homebody, resident; settled

**8.** bloodless

**9.** net; partial; delicate, fine; thin; petty

**10.** stiff, rigid, wooden; to stiffen

**11.** to enlighten, set straight

**12.** to foster, promote, nourish, encourage

**13.** to prevent, deter, hinder

**14.** unfriendly, ill-humored, gruff, hostile

**15.** retirement, departure

**Choosing the Right Word**  *Encircle the **boldface** word that more satisfactorily completes each of the following sentences.*

1. The disc jockey promised to (**vacate, debut**) the band's long-awaited new album as soon as it was released by the record company.

2. Many a student dreams about spending a (**vagabond, partisan**) year idly hitchhiking through Europe.

3. One of the biggest problems facing the United States today is how to stop the (**blight, leeway**) that is creeping over large parts of our great cities.

4. Poland received top priority on Adolf Hitler's (**agenda, maze**) of military conquests in the fall of 1939.

5. In her graphic description of the most gruesome scenes in the horror film, Maria left out none of the (**amiable, gory**) details.

6. Over the years, so many of the columnist's predictions have come true that he is now looked on as something of a(n) (**partisan, oracle**).

7. As we moved higher up the mountain, I was overcome by dizziness and fatigue (**induced, vacated**) by the thin air.

8. Since he is an expert gymnast and works out every day, his body has remained as (**limber, compliant**) as that of a boy.

9. Students must take many required courses, but they also have a little (**maze, leeway**) to choose courses that they find especially interesting.

10. What I thought was going to be a(n) (**amiable, partisan**) little chat with my boss soon turned into a real donnybrook.

11. Don't let the (**clarity, leeway**) of the water fool you into supposing that it's safe for drinking.

12. If you want to get a clear picture of just what went wrong, you must not (**induce, befuddle**) your mind with all kinds of wild rumors.

13. This matter is so important to all the people of the community that we must forget (**partisan, boisterous**) politics and work together.

14. At the end of the long series of discussions and arguments, we felt that we were trapped in a (**blight, maze**) of conflicting ideas and plans.

15. After all the deductions had been made from my (**gross, amiable**) salary, the sum that remained seemed pitifully small.

16. Miss Roth, the librarian, cracks down hard on (**compliant, boisterous**) students.

17. The landlord ordered all tenants to (**vacate, reimburse**) the premises by noon.

18. An experienced backpacker can give you many useful suggestions for (**limbering, conserving**) energy on a long, tough hike.

19. Because she is usually so (**compliant, partisan**), we were all surprised when she said that she didn't like our plans and wouldn't accept them.

20. I will feel fully (**reimbursed, conserved**) for all that I have done for her if I can see her in good health again.

# Review  Units 4–6

**Analogies**  *In each of the following, encircle the item that best completes the comparison.*

**1. hero** is to **idolize** as
a. partisan is to ignore
b. inhabitant is to reimburse
c. buddy is to discredit
d. villain is to despise

**2. mortal** is to **death** as
a. acute is to decay
b. fluid is to change
c. permanent is to duration
d. elusive is to time

**3. dancer** is to **limber** as
a. pickpocket is to smug
b. loudmouth is to boisterous
c. showoff is to acute
d. spoilsport is to amiable

**4. bulldozer** is to **topple** as
a. derrick is to blight
b. plow is to devastate
c. crane is to raise
d. truck is to conserve

**5. hungry** is to **ravenous** as
a. tired is to exhausted
b. sleepy is to awake
c. thirsty is to drunk
d. dirty is to spotless

**6. inhabitant** is to **live** as
a. resident is to leave
b. employee is to own
c. guest is to dwell
d. tourist is to visit

**7. vagabond** is to **wander** as
a. beggar is to explore
b. nomad is to tarry
c. drifter is to roam
d. homebody is to travel

**8. mule** is to **headstrong** as
a. lamb is to compliant
b. wolf is to amiable
c. horse is to numb
d. mouse is to boisterous

**9. acquit** is to **innocence** as
a. arrest is to blamelessness
b. convict is to guilt
c. clear is to complicity
d. release is to suspicion

**10. numb** is to **feel** as
a. paralyzed is to move
b. injured is to hear
c. blind is to taste
d. lame is to see

**11. loyal** is to **fidelity** as
a. intelligent is to stupidity
b. brave is to cowardice
c. thankful is to gratitude
d. ignorant is to wisdom

**12. repent** is to **remorse** as
a. desire is to hatred
b. enjoy is to anxiety
c. fear is to pleasure
d. boast is to pride

**13. scan** is to **eye** as
a. observe is to ear
b. touch is to finger
c. smell is to mouth
d. taste is to nose

**14. gross** is to **refinement** as
a. boisterous is to noise
b. smug is to contentment
c. amiable is to friendliness
d. petty is to significance

**15. liquor** is to **befuddle** as
a. coffee is to stimulate
b. tea is to deem
c. water is to generate
d. milk is to induce

**16. gory** is to **blood** as
a. dull is to interest
b. eerie is to mystery
c. pale is to color
d. numb is to sensation

**17. devastate** is to **ruined** as
a. conserve is to musty
b. blight is to soggy
c. bungle is to noisy
d. vacate is to empty

**18. clarity** is to **clear** as
a. simplicity is to complicated
b. charm is to boring
c. brevity is to short
d. force is to weak

**Definitions**    *In each of the following groups, encircle the word that is best defined or suggested by the introductory phrase.*

**1.** to look over quickly
a. scan          b. generate          c. bungle          d. discredit

**2.** one who lives in a particular place
a. leeway          b. commentary          c. inhabitant          d. keepsake

**3.** friendly and pleasant
a. elusive          b. amiable          c. limber          d. gross

**4.** condition of being lost in thought
a. remorse          b. reverie          c. strand          d. maze

**5.** bringing about death
a. headstrong          b. blight          c. mortal          d. ravenous

**6.** to find not guilty of a charge
a. induce          b. devastate          c. idolize          d. acquit

**7.** showing great insight or sharpness
a. acute          b. gory          c. numb          d. smug

**8.** to pay back
a. repent          b. reimburse          c. debut          d. refute

**9.** to throw doubt or uncertainty on
a. idolize          b. fray          c. conserve          d. discredit

**10.** one who speaks with wisdom and authority
a. inhabitant          b. partisan          c. oracle          d. mortal

**11.** length of time that something lasts
a. leeway          b. duration          c. clarity          d. ovation

**12.** to show sorrow for bad conduct
a. repent          b. tarry          c. generate          d. bluster

**13.** state of being faithful
a. revocation          b. synopsis          c. maze          d. fidelity

**14.** to make a first appearance in public
a. strife          b. setback          c. debut          d. agenda

**15.** loud and noisy
a. boisterous          b. compliant          c. eerie          d. petty

**16.** to bring about someone's downfall
a. deem          b. topple          c. vacate          d. pacify

**17.** series of notes explaining a book
a. commentary          b. facet          c. plight          d. ingratitude

**18.** deep regret for some past misdeed
a. strand          b. agenda          c. bluster          d. remorse

**19.** to confuse or bewilder
a. tarry          b. befuddle          c. scan          d. fray

**20.** wanderer or tramp
a. partisan          b. inhabitant          c. vagabond          d. keepsake

**Shades of Meaning**    *Read each sentence carefully. Then encircle the item that best completes the statement below the sentence.*

At Dunkirk in the Spring of 1940 an armada of warships and civilian craft evacuated hundreds of thousands of Allied soldiers from the Normandy strand, where they had been encircled by the German army. **(2)**

**1.** In line 3 the word **strand** most nearly means
a. fiber
b. shore
c. abandonment
d. battle

On June 30, 1971, the Supreme Court vacated a lower court's restraining order, thus freeing newspapers to resume publication of the Pentagon Papers. **(2)**

**2.** The best definition for the word **vacated** in line 1 is
a. annulled/voided
b. deserted
c. emptied
d. gave up

Skyscrapers of the 1930s, such as the Empire State Building and the Chrysler Building in New York, typically are crowned with setbacks that lead like steps to a spire at the summit. **(2)**

**3.** The word **setbacks** in line 2 is best defined as
a. defeats
b. reversals
c. disappointments
d. recesses

The commentator's petty evaluation of the election results betrays a woeful ignorance of American political history. **(2)**

**4.** In line 1 the word **petty** most nearly means
a. unimportant
b. minor
c. narrow-minded
d. insignificant

The fellow is so off-putting and mean that I am sure he must count his enemies by the gross. **(2)**

**5.** The word **gross** in line 2 is used to mean
a. total
b. twelve dozen
c. weight
d. score

---

**Antonyms**    *In each of the following groups, encircle the word or expression that is most nearly **opposite** in meaning to the word in **boldface type** in the introductory phrase.*

**1. idolize** the star
a. hate      b. bore      c. train      d. deceive

**2.** my friend's **ingratitude**
a. wisdom      b. trust      c. thankfulness      d. money

**3. boisterous** fans
a. noisy      b. numerous      c. foreign      d. quiet

**4.** an **acute** pain
a. strange      b. dull      c. new      d. sharp

**5.** **limber** muscles
a. stiff      b. large      c. tiny      d. loose

**6.** evidence that **refutes** the charge
a. disproves      b. lessens      c. confirms      d. changes

**7.** **vacate** an apartment
a. own      b. paint      c. clean      d. occupy

**8.** **conserve** energy
a. store      b. waste      c. purchase      d. save

**9.** a **petty** concern
a. small      b. weird      c. important      d. new

**10.** a major **setback**
a. advance      b. defeat      c. problem      d. effort

**11.** a **headstrong** fellow
a. neat      b. intelligent      c. wealthy      d. docile

**12.** a time of **strife**
a. harmony      b. unemployment      c. plenty      d. trouble

**13.** an **amiable** companion
a. brilliant      b. tall      c. gruff      d. rich

**14.** don't wish to **tarry** here
a. stay      b. leave      c. eat      d. loiter

**15.** to **devastate** a region
a. inhabit      b. liberate      c. develop      d. conquer

---

**Completing the Sentence**

*From the following lists of words, choose the one that best completes each of the sentences below. Write the word in the space provided.*

**Group A**

| | | | |
|---|---|---|---|
| plight | partisan | elusive | idolize |
| petty | facet | ovation | deem |

**1.** Bea has many good qualities, but the one _____ of her personality that I admire most is her sincerity.

**2.** Though many in Lincoln's cabinet privately scorned General McClellan, the soldiers of the Army of the Potomac practically _____ the "Young Napoleon."

**3.** The idea is so _____ that just when I think I understand it, I get confused all over again.

**4.** I _____ it to be the height of bad taste to boast about your family's wealth.

**5.** She is such a brilliant speaker that the audience usually gives her a standing _____ at the end of her talks.

*Group B*

| | | | |
|---|---|---|---|
| **strand** | **discredit** | **ravenous** | **debut** |
| **fray** | **eerie** | **leeway** | **blight** |
| **duration** | **reverie** | **maze** | **generate** |

**1.** Since we can't expect everyone to be 100% accurate, we must allow some _____ for human error.

**2.** When we got to that crossing, with a three-way light and roads leading in every direction, we felt as though we were in a(n) _____ .

**3.** Instead of standing on the sidelines and explaining what everyone is doing wrong, why don't you get into the _____ yourself?

**4.** A mysterious _____ destroyed the better part of the corn crop, causing widespread famine and hardship.

**5.** Since I hadn't had a bite to eat all day, I was _____ by dinnertime.

---

**Word Families**

**A.** *On the line provided, write a* **noun form** *of each of the following words.*

EXAMPLE: petty — **pettiness**

**1.** eerie _____

**2.** smug _____

**3.** amiable _____

**4.** compliant _____

**5.** gory _____

**6.** acquit _____

**7.** devastate _____

**8.** repent _____

**9.** pacify _____

**10.** befuddle _____

**11.** induce _____

**12.** conserve _____

**13.** idolize _____

**14.** gross _____

**15.** reimburse _____

**R**

**B.** *On the line provided, write a **verb** related to each of the following words.*

EXAMPLE: inhabitant — **inhabit**

1. elusive _____

2. compliant _____

3. revocation _____

4. commentary _____

5. duration _____

6. clarity _____

---

**Filling the Blanks**

*Encircle the pair of words that best complete each of the following passages.*

1. The defense was able to _____ the prosecution's case so convincingly that the jury _____ the defendant after only five minutes of deliberation.

   a. devastate . . . befuddled     c. topple . . . discredited
   b. refute . . . acquitted     d. bungled . . . reimbursed

2. In the third century, bands of savage barbarians repeatedly broke through the frontier defenses of the Roman province of Gaul, _____ the countryside with fire and sword, and either slew or carried off the

   _____ .

   a. scanned . . . partisans     c. devastated . . . inhabitants
   b. pacified . . . vagabonds     d. blighted . . . oracles

3. "The Scholar Gypsy" tells the tale of a poor student who left school to join a band of _____ . He and his companions roamed the countryside endlessly, never _____ in one place for long.

   a. inhabitants . . . deeming     c. partisans . . . generating
   b. debutants . . . vacating     d. vagabonds . . . tarrying

4. When the new government came to power, its first order of business was to _____ a country that had been torn by _____ and revolution for over ten years.

   a. pacify . . . strife     c. strand . . . fidelity
   b. topple . . . ingratitude     d. conserve . . . remorse

5. The TV special not only brought in huge sums of money to help relieve the _____ of millions of Africans suffering from the effects of a severe famine but also _____ a great deal of sympathy for them.

   a. setback . . . induced     c. duration . . . deemed
   b. plight . . . generated     d. strife . . . conserved

# Cumulative Review   Units 1–6

**Analogies**   *In each of the following, choose the item that best completes the comparison.*

**1. elusive** is to **grasp** as
a. hazy is to see
b. spicy is to taste
c. sharp is to smell
d. loud is to hear

**2. compress** is to **swelling** as
a. splint is to snakebite
b. bandage is to broken leg
c. steak is to black eye
d. crutch is to bloody nose

**3. messenger** is to **dispatch** as
a. partisan is to synopsis
b. oracle is to prophecy
c. bigot is to keepsake
d. oaf is to ovation

**4. gloat** is to **satisfaction** as
a. repent is to regret
b. forsake is to delight
c. confront is to fear
d. idolize is to amusement

**5. irk** is to **annoyance** as
a. befuddle is to understanding
b. ruffle is to joy
c. infuriate is to rage
d. pacify is to discontent

**6. hairline** is to **recede** as
a. city is to besiege
b. tide is to ebb
c. building is to topple
d. task is to bungle

**7. illusion** is to **deceive** as
a. enigma is to mystify
b. vow is to devastate
c. repast is to disturb
d. leeway is to restrict

**8. famished** is to **ravenous** as
a. contemporary is to prehistoric
b. global is to aquatic
c. frozen is to numb
d. stiff is to limber

**9. fray** is to **boisterous** as
a. skyscraper is to petty
b. ocean is to arid
c. tempest is to sheepish
d. massacre is to gory

**10. eerie** is to **ghosts** as
a. frightening is to monsters
b. elusive is to cowboys
c. incomprehensible is to clowns
d. sage is to spies

---

**Shades of Meaning**   *Read each sentence carefully. Then encircle the item that best completes the statement below the sentence.*

The naturalist and author John Burroughs (1837–1921) was one of the first to advocate the conservation of our country's natural resources.   **(2)**

**1.** In line 2 the word **conservation** is best defined as
a. waste
b. study
c. supervision
d. preservation

Of Silvia, in *Two Gentlemen of Verona,* Shakespeare has the players sing, "She excels each mortal thing upon the dull earth dwelling."   **(2)**

**2.** The word **mortal** in line 2 most nearly means
a. often deadly
b. potentially fatal
c. usually lethal
d. certain to die

The new management introduced a number of cost-cutting measures designed to wring a maximum of profit from the struggling business.   **(2)**

**3.** The word **maximum** in line 2 is best defined as
a. greatest possible amount
b. modest amount
c. least possible amount
d. record level

Their disinterested expressions suggested that many of the soldiers returning from the front were suffering the effects of battle fatigue. (2)

**4.** In line 1 the word **disinterested** most nearly means
 a. apathetic
 b. impartial
 c. unselfish
 d. frightened

A truly gifted mimic can adopt not only another's voice but that person's expressions and mannerisms as well. (2)

**5.** The word **mimic** in line 1 is best defined as
 a. comedian
 b. imitator
 c. magician
 d. ventriloquist

---

**Filling
the Blanks**   *Encircle the pair of words that best complete the meaning of each of the following passages.*

**1.** During the ten years that he spent conquering Gaul, Julius Caesar wrote a series of _____ on his campaigns. In these accounts, he not only tells the story of the war but also _____ the daily life and customs of the peoples he subdued.
 a. reveries . . .conserves
 b. barrages . . . discredits
 c. commentarioo . . . depicts
 d. mazes . . . designates

**2.** On that cold and _____ November morning, the sails on our boat _____ and flapped in the wind like so many sheets on a giant clothesline.
 a. serene . . . constrained
 b. blustery . . . billowed
 c. eerie . . . generated
 d. adverse . . . tarried

**3.** The linesman's adverse calls so _____ one of the players in the championship match that he began to shower the unfortunate official with an angry _____ of verbal abuse.
 a. infuriated . . . barrage
 b. pacified . . . dispatch
 c. motivated . . . queue
 d. befuddled . . . strand

**4.** When a series of natural disasters turned their once fertile valley into a "dust bowl," the _____ of the area _____ their homes and sought a more hospitable environment in which to live.
 a. partisans . . . denounced
 b. oafs . . . devastated
 c. hypocrites . . . vacated
 d. inhabitants . . . forsook

**5.** "Though I didn't expect to be _____ in any monetary way for the help I'd given them," I replied, "I was totally taken aback by their complete lack of _____ for what I'd done."
 a. irked . . . remorse
 b. reimbursed . . . gratitude
 c. confronted . . . clarity
 d. befuddled . . . diversity

# Unit 7

**Definitions**

Note carefully the spelling, pronunciation, and definition of each of the following words. Then write the word in the blank space in the illustrative phrase following.

**1. authorize**
('ô thə rīz)

(v.) to approve or permit; to give power or authority to

_____ her to sign the contract

**2. booty**
('büt ē)

(n.) plunder; spoils taken (as from an enemy in war); anything valuable obtained by force or dishonesty

divided the _____

**3. culprit**
('kəl prit)

(n.) a person who has committed a crime or is guilty of some misconduct; an offender

catch the _____ red-handed

**4. dawdle**
('dôd əl)

(v.) to waste time; to be idle; to spend more time in doing something than is necessary

_____ over the job

**5. dissect**
(di 'sekt)

(v.) to cut apart in preparation for scientific study; to analyze with great care

_____ the frog in the lab

**6. expend**
(ek 'spend)

(v.) to pay out, spend; to use up

_____ their energy in vain

**7. fatality**
(fā 'tal ə tē)

(n.) an event resulting in death; an accidental death

a traffic _____

**8. gullible**
('gəl ə bəl)

(adj.) easily fooled, tricked, or cheated

_____ enough to believe anything

**9. illicit**
(i 'lis it)

(adj.) not permitted, unlawful, improper

_____ drugs

**10. immerse**
(i 'mərs)

(v.) to plunge or dip into a fluid; to involve deeply, absorb

completely _____ in his work

**11. inflammatory**
(in 'flam ə tôr ē)

(adj.) causing excitement or anger; leading to violence or disorder

an _____ speech

**12. memorandum**
(mem ə 'ran dəm)

(n.) a note to aid one's memory; an informal note or report (pl., memorandums or memoranda)

a _____ on school problems

**13. pathetic**
(pə 'thet ik)

(adj.) marked by strong emotion, especially pity and sorrow; able to move people emotionally; worthy of pity; woefully inadequate

a _____ sight

55

**14. persevere** (v.) to keep doing something in spite of difficulties; to
(pər sə 'vēr) refuse to quit even when the going is tough

_____ in working toward our goals

**15. prevaricate** (v.) to lie, tell an untruth; to mislead on purpose
(pri 'var ə kāt)
an unfortunate tendency to _____

**16. quash** (v.) to crush, put down completely
(kwäsh)
_____ the revolt

**17. relish** (n.) enjoyment or satisfaction; something that adds a
('rel ish) pleasing flavor; (v.) to enjoy greatly

ate the meal with great _____

**18. reminisce** (v.) to recall one's past thoughts, feelings, or
(rem ə 'nis) experiences

_____ about last year's canoe trip

**19. scour** (v.) to clean or polish by hard rubbing; to examine with
(skaür) great care; to move about quickly in search of

_____ the pots and pans

**20. writhe** (v.) to make twisting or turning movements in a way that
(rīth) suggests pain or struggle

_____ like a sidewinder

---

**Completing the Sentence**  Choose the word from this unit that best completes each of the following sentences. Write it in the space given.

1. It is said that the pirates of old buried their _____ on small islands in the Caribbean Sea.

2. The children won't _____ over their homework if they know they'll be getting cheese and crackers as soon as they finish.

3. Cracking down on _____ drug traffic is one of the biggest problems facing law-enforcement agencies in the United States.

4. We tried to hold Tom steady, but he _____ with pain as the doctor put splints on his broken leg.

5. I love to listen to my grandfather _____ about his boyhood adventures in Coney Island.

6. No matter how talented you may be, you will never be successful unless you learn to _____ in what you undertake.

7. "Only a bigot would dare to make such a rude and _____ remark, even in jest," I replied.

8. Many people were injured in the explosion, but luckily there was not a single _____ .

**9.** After we had _____ the animal, we had to point to each of its important organs and explain its main function.

**10.** The story of the homeless child was so _____ that it moved us all to tears.

**11.** The dictator ordered his secret police to _____ any attempt to organize a protest rally.

**12.** Our supervisor prepared a(n) _____ that reminded the sales-people of the procedures to be followed during the holiday season.

**13.** We had to _____ the walls for hours to get rid of the dirt and grease with which they were encrusted.

**14.** This pass _____ you to visit certain rooms in this museum that are not open to the general public.

**15.** You may not _____ being told that your carelessness was responsible for the accident, but that happens to be true.

**16.** Because he was seen near the scene of the crime at the time the deed

was committed, he was suspected of being the _____ .

**17.** Is it wise to _____ so much of your hard-earned money on things that you don't really want or need?

**18.** Before you _____ yourself in the bath, be sure to test the temperature of the water.

**19.** You may be tempted to _____ , but in the long run it will be to your advantage to own up to the truth about your unfortunate error.

**20.** Do you really think that I am _____ enough to believe his foolish story about being a member of the Olympic team?

---

**Synonyms**      *Choose the word from this unit that is most nearly **the same** in meaning as each of the following groups of expressions. Write the word on the line given.*

**1.** moving, distressing, pitiable, heartrending      _____

**2.** overtrusting, innocent, naive, credulous      _____

**3.** to crush, suppress      _____

**4.** to cut apart, analyze, examine      _____

**5.** to plug away, pursue, stick to it      _____

**6.** a casualty, mortality      _____

**7.** to fib, stretch the truth, equivocate      _____

**8.** to spend, consume, use up; to disburse      _____

**9.** provoking, incendiary, provocative      _____

**10.** to order, entitle, empower; to approve  _____

**11.** to twist, squirm, thrash  _____

**12.** to delay, loiter, dillydally  _____

**13.** to dip, plunge, dunk; to engross  _____

**14.** a reminder, note  _____

**15.** illegal, unlawful, unauthorized, forbidden  _____

**16.** to remember, recollect, recall  _____

**17.** pleasure, gusto; to take delight in  _____

**18.** loot, plunder, spoils  _____

**19.** to scrub, polish; to search, comb  _____

**20.** an offender, lawbreaker, wrongdoer  _____

---

**Antonyms**  *Choose the word from this unit that is most nearly **opposite** in meaning to each of the following groups of expressions. Write the word on the line given.*

**1.** legal, lawful, permissible, aboveboard  _____

**2.** to tell the truth  _____

**3.** to give up, despair, throw in the towel  _____

**4.** suspicious, skeptical  _____

**5.** to hurry, hasten, speed up, bustle  _____

**6.** to dirty, soil  _____

**7.** to save, hoard  _____

**8.** to dredge up, pull out  _____

**9.** funny, hilarious; frightening  _____

**10.** calming, soothing, lulling, quieting  _____

**11.** to dislike, loathe, hate, despise  _____

**12.** to start, kindle, ignite, encourage  _____

**13.** to forbid, ban, prohibit  _____

**14.** an injury  _____

**15.** to sew together, fuse, weld  _____

**Choosing the Right Word**   *Encircle the **boldface** word that more satisfactorily completes each of the following sentences.*

1. The more he tried to protect himself by (**scouring, prevaricating**), the more he became entrapped in his own web of lies.

2. She (**expends, dawdles**) so much time and energy on small matters that she can't prepare properly for the things that are really important to her.

3. Is there any sight more (**pathetic, inflammatory**) than a lonely old person peering out of a tenement window hour after hour?

4. His scheme to make money by preparing term papers for other students is not only completely (**gullible, illicit**) but immoral as well.

5. When the class comedian imitated my way of speaking, it was all I could do not to (**writhe, relish**) with embarrassment.

6. When it became known that four explorers were lost in the jungle, special search parties were sent out to (**expend, scour**) the area for them.

7. We were amazed at the (**booty, relish**) that Edna brought home just for answering a few questions on the TV quiz show.

8. It was plain from the way that he (**dawdled, expended**) over breakfast that he was in no hurry to visit the dentist.

9. Since the charges against the suspected mugger will probably not hold up in court, the district attorney has decided to (**authorize, quash**) them.

10. No one (**relishes, immerses**) being reminded of his or her mistakes, but if you are wise you will try to benefit from such criticism.

11. Although our coach can spend hours (**reminiscing, writhing**) about his victories, he doesn't have an equally good memory for his defeats.

12. She was so deeply (**immersed, expended**) in the book she was reading that she did not even hear us enter the room.

13. In spite of all that you say about how hard it is to get into medical school, I intend to (**persevere, relish**) in my plans to become a doctor.

14. His sticky fingers and the crumbs around his mouth convinced us that he was the (**culprit, booty**) in the Case of the Empty Cookie Jar.

15. With the skill of a trained debater, she (**prevaricated, dissected**) her opponent's arguments one by one to reveal their basic weaknesses.

16. I am afraid that our ambitious plan to modernize the gym has become a (**memorandum, fatality**) of the School Board's economy drive.

17. She is so worried about appearing (**inflammatory, gullible**) that she sometimes refuses to believe things that are well supported by facts.

18. What good does it do for the president of the Student Council to issue (**fatalities, memorandums**) if no one takes the trouble to read them?

19. Dictators like Hitler and Mussolini used (**pathetic, inflammatory**) language to stir up the emotions of the crowds they addressed.

20. We learned in our social studies class that the Constitution (**dissects, authorizes**) the President to arrange treaties with foreign countries.

**Definitions** *Note carefully the spelling, pronunciation, and definition of each of the following words. Then write the word in the blank space in the illustrative phrase following.*

**1. affluence**
('af lü əns)

(*n.*) wealth, riches, prosperity, great abundance

from poverty to _____

**2. arrears**
(ə 'rērz)

(*n., pl.*) unpaid and overdue debts; an unfinished duty

found himself deep in _____

**3. cascade**
(kas 'kād)

(*n.*) a steep, narrow waterfall; something falling or rushing forth in quantity; (*v.*) to flow downward (like a waterfall)

_____ down the mountainside

**4. cringe**
(krinj)

(*v.*) to shrink back or hide in fear or submissiveness

_____ at the sight

**5. crotchety**
('kräch ə tē)

(*adj.*) cranky, ill-tempered; full of odd whims

a _____ boss

**6. format**
('fôr mat)

(*n.*) the size, shape, or arrangement of something

the _____ of a newspaper

**7. immobile**
(i 'mō bəl)

(*adj.*) not movable; not moving

remain _____ for hours

**8. impassable**
(im 'pas ə bəl)

(*adj.*) blocked so that nothing can go through

an _____ barrier

**9. innovation**
(i nō 'vā shən)

(*n.*) something new, a change; the act of introducing a new method, idea, device, etc.

an energy-saving _____

**10. jovial**
('jō vē əl)

(*adj.*) good-humored, in high spirits; merry

a _____ personality

**11. manacle**
('man ə kəl)

(*n., usually pl.*) a handcuff, anything that chains or confines; (*v.*) to chain or restrain (as with handcuffs)

_____ the prisoner

**12. martial**
('mär shəl)

(*adj.*) warlike, fond of fighting; relating to war, the army, or military life

_____ law

**13. minimum**
('min ə məm)

(*n.*) the smallest possible amount; (*adj.*) the lowest permissible or possible

meet the _____ requirements

**14. nimble**
('nim bəl)

(*adj.*) quick and skillful in movement, agile; clever

a dancer's _____ feet

60

**15. onset**
('än set)

(n.) the beginning, start (especially of something violent and destructive); an attack, assault

the _____ of the storm

**16. partition**
(pär 'tish ən)

(n.) something that divides (such as a wall); the act of dividing something into parts or sections; (v.) to divide into parts or shares

separated by a wooden _____

**17. perishable**
('per ə shə bəl)

(adj.) likely to spoil or decay

kept the _____ foods chilled

**18. retrieve**
(ri 'trēv)

(v.) to find and bring back, get back, recover; to put right, make good

_____ the ball

**19. sinister**
('sin ə stər)

(adj.) appearing evil or dangerous; threatening evil or harm

a _____ development

**20. taut**
(tôt)

(adj.) tightly drawn, tense; neat, in good order

drew the rope _____

---

**Completing the Sentence**

*Choose the word from this unit that best completes each of the following sentences. Write it in the space given.*

1. I was able to _____ my baggage promptly after leaving the plane.

2. During the war years, the government tried by all kinds of propaganda to arouse the _____ spirit of the people.

3. The more we tried to humor the _____ crossing guard, the more irritable and demanding he seemed to become.

4. Unless you pull the ropes _____ , the tennis net will sag.

5. It's a pleasure to watch the _____ fingers of the expert typist as they move swiftly over the keyboard.

6. I don't expect you to be a hero, but do you have to _____ in that cowardly fashion whenever anyone so much as disagrees with you?

7. The sunlight caught the waters of the stream as they _____ over the steep cliff and formed a brilliant rainbow.

8. We made use of _____ to break up the floor space into a large number of small offices.

9. His back injury was so severe that he has been placed in a cast and will have to remain _____ for months.

**10.** Frank Lloyd Wright was a great American architect who was responsible for many _____ in the design of buildings.

**11.** The patients will have a much better chance to recover quickly if they receive treatment at the first _____ of the fever.

**12.** The _____ mood of our cheerful little gathering changed abruptly to sorrow when news of the tragedy came over the radio.

**13.** We plan to change the _____ of our school magazine to make it more attractive and readable.

**14.** As a result of the record-breaking snowstorm, all roads in the area became

_____ .

**15.** Today _____ foods are shipped in refrigerated trucks to prevent spoilage.

**16.** I know that my payments on the car are in _____ , but I will catch up as soon as I get my next paycheck.

**17.** Can you explain why there is not only a maximum speed limit but also a(n) _____ speed limit on many modern highways?

**18.** Sherlock Holmes detected in the wicked scheme the _____ hand of the evil Professor Moriarty.

**19.** The feeling of _____ I had when I was paid lasted only until I had finished taking care of my bills.

**20.** Although we are sure that the prisoners will make no attempt to escape, the law requires us to place _____ on them.

---

**Synonyms**    *Choose the word from this unit that is most nearly **the same** in meaning as each of the following groups of expressions. Write the word on the line given.*

**1.** to recover, regain; to fetch                 _____

**2.** closed, blocked, impenetrable             _____

**3.** military, warlike, hostile, bellicose       _____

**4.** the outset, beginning, commencement    _____

**5.** frightening, menacing, ominous           _____

**6.** fixed, stationary, unmoving, rooted       _____

**7.** a handcuff; to put in chains, fetter       _____

**8.** in default, in the red; late, overdue       _____

**9.** subject to decay, short-lived, fleeting    _____

**10.** jolly, merry, cheerful, festive

**11.** a waterfall; to plunge, rush, tumble

**12.** a change, modernization; a new wrinkle

**13.** wealth, prosperity; plenty, abundance

**14.** a divider, separation; to subdivide

**15.** grouchy, crabby, cranky; eccentric

**16.** a shape, arrangement, layout, design

**17.** quick, lively, agile; keen, clever; flexible

**18.** to flinch, duck, shrink, cower; to fawn

**19.** tight, strained; orderly, shipshape

**20.** the least possible; smallest, least

---

**Antonyms**    *Choose the word from this unit that is most nearly* **opposite** *in meaning to each of the following groups of expressions. Write the word on the line given.*

**1.** to strut, swagger

**2.** to join, combine, consolidate, merge

**3.** unblocked, clear, open, fit for travel

**4.** the maximum; highest, most

**5.** awkward, clumsy; stiff, inflexible

**6.** long-lasting, durable; undying, permanent

**7.** gloomy, morose, melancholy, cheerless

**8.** a drip, drop; to trickle, ooze

**9.** poverty, want, destitution; scarcity

**10.** sociable, friendly, agreeable, amiable

**11.** the conclusion, close, end

**12.** movable, portable; nimble, agile

**13.** peace-loving, peaceable, pacific, unwarlike

**14.** cheering, encouraging, reassuring; benign

**15.** to unchain, set free, emancipate, release

**16.** loose, slack, drooping; messy, sloppy

**Choosing the Right Word**   *Encircle the **boldface** word that more satisfactorily completes each of the following sentences.*

1. Despite all his efforts, he was never able to (**retrieve, partition**) the fine reputation he had lost by that crooked deal.

2. We learned in our history class that the ancient Romans were very fine soldiers and excelled in all the (**martial, perishable**) arts.

3. The self-styled "tough guy" (**cringed, manacled**) in terror and begged the police not to shoot.

4. In the moment of danger, my nerves were so (**taut, perishable**) that I would have screamed if someone had touched me.

5. Normally, I'm very even tempered, but I can become a little (**crotchety, martial**) when I'm tired or hungry.

6. Her shimmering blond hair fell upon her pretty shoulders like a(n) (**onset, cascade**) of gold.

7. Instead of acting as though you were permanently (**manacled, retrieved**) to your small circle of friends, you should try to meet new people.

8. Although we are proud of our high living standard, we should not forget that there are those who do not share in this (**affluence, cascade**).

9. If you spend much time watching TV, you will come to realize that all the news programs share the same basic (**format, minimum**).

10. Although we all recognize that there must be changes, it is a mistake to think that every (**arrears, innovation**) is necessarily an improvement.

11. In the 18th century, Russia, Prussia, and Austria made a series of deals to (**partition, cringe**) and annex Poland right out of existence.

12. Her mind is so (**impassable, nimble**) that she always seems to be one step ahead of us in any matter under discussion.

13. A high school student looking for a vacation job usually can't expect to earn more than the (**perishable, minimum**) wage.

14. With the (**affluence, onset**) of the heat wave, vast numbers of city dwellers began to stream toward the beaches and mountains.

15. Of all the different types of writing, humor may be the most (**perishable, jovial**) because each generation has its own idea of what is funny.

16. The first thing the bankrupt firm must do with what funds it has is pay the (**arrears, formats**) due on the employees' wages.

17. The speed with which the boxer darted about the ring made his lumbering, opponent seem utterly (**nimble, immobile**) by comparison.

18. Robin Hood's faithful band of merry men were not only (**crotchety, jovial**) companions, but brave fighters as well.

19. I felt that there was something thoroughly (**sinister, immobile**) about the way he kept trying to duck questions on that subject.

20. More than once, our nimble running backs managed to find a way through our opponents' supposedly (**impassable, affluent**) line.

# Unit 9

**Definitions**

*Note carefully the spelling, pronunciation, and definition of each of the following words. Then write the word in the blank space in the illustrative phrase following.*

**1. avenge**
(ə ′venj)

(*v.*) to get revenge for; to punish someone or get satisfaction for a wrong or injury

_____ the massacre

**2. cede** \
(sēd)

(*v.*) to give up; surrender; to hand over to another

_____ the land to the state

**3. deluge** ı
(′del yüj)

(*n.*) a great flood; a heavy fall of rain; anything that comes in vast quantity (like a flood); (*v.*) to flood

a _____ of visitors

**4. discretion** ı
(dis ′kresh ən)

(*n.*) good judgment; care in speech and action; freedom to judge or choose

leave it to your _____

**5. giddy** ⁄
(′gid ē)

(*adj.*) dizzy; light-headed; lacking seriousness

felt _____ and light-headed

**6. impact** ⁄
(*n.*, ′im pakt;
*v.*, im ′pakt)

(*n.*) the striking of one object against another; the shock caused by a collision; (*v.*) to affect, especially forcefully

the _____ of the blow

**7. intimidate** ⁄
(in ′tim ə dāt)

(*v.*) to make timid or frighten by threats; to use fear to get someone to do (or not to do) something

_____ us with threats

**8. liberate**
(′lib ə rāt)

(*v.*) to free from bondage or domination; to release

_____ the prisoners

**9. logical** ı
(′läj ə kəl)

(*adj.*) reasonable; making use of reason and good sense

a _____ solution to the problem

**10. misrepresent** \
(mis rep ri ′zent)

(*v.*) to give a false or untrue idea

_____ the facts

**11. optional** ⁄
(′äp shə nəl)

(*adj.*) left to one's own choice; not required

an _____ course

**12. outright** ⁄
(′aut rīt)

(*adj.*) complete; instantaneous; without reservation, thoroughgoing; (*adv.*) completely; instantaneously

an _____ lie

**13. rendezvous** \
(′rän dā vü)

(*v.*) to meet in accordance with a plan; (*n.*) a meeting by agreement; a meeting place

plan to _____ at six o'clock

**14. rotund** \
(rō ′tənd)

(*adj.*) rounded and plump; full or rich in sound

as smooth and _____ as a ball

**15. saunter**
(′sôn tər)

(*v.*) to stroll; walk in an easy, leisurely way; (*n.*) a stroll

_____ through the park

**16. sluggish** \
(′sləg ish)

(*adj.*) lazy; slow-moving; not active, dull

a _____ current

**17. subordinate**
(*v.*, sə ′bôr də nāt;
*adj.*, *n.*, sə ′bôr
də nət)

(*adj.*) lower in rank or position, secondary; (*n.*) one who is in a lower position or under the orders of someone else; (*v.*) to put in a lower or secondary position

a _____ officer

**18. tint**
(tint)

(*n.*) a delicate color or hue; a slight trace of something; (*v.*) to give color to something; to dye

glasses that are _____

**19. variable**
(′vâr ē ə bəl)

(*adj.*) likely to undergo change; changeable; (*n.*) a value or quantity that varies; a symbol for such

extremely _____ weather

**20. verge**
(vərj)

(*n.*) the point at which something begins or happens; the brink; a border, edge; (*v.*) to incline, tend toward; to be in the process of becoming something else

on the _____ of disaster

---

**Completing the Sentence**

*Choose the word from this unit that best completes each of the following sentences. Write it in the space given.*

1. Her argument was so _____ that she convinced us that her solution to the math problem was the correct one.

2. After being defeated in a war that lasted from 1846 to 1848, Mexico was forced to _____ vast territories to the United States.

3. We believe that the world is now on the _____ of new and exciting developments that may dramatically change the way we live.

4. By late September the leaves on the trees in my neck of the woods have begun to take on their normal autumn _____ .

5. The two groups of hikers, setting out from different points, have planned a(n) _____ at four o'clock at Eagle Rock.

6. You may like to live where the sun shines all the time, but I prefer a more _____ climate.

7. Because of the lawyer's long experience in legal matters, we left it to his _____ how to proceed with the case.

**8.** According to the Bible, Noah and his family were the only human beings to survive the great _____ _____ that once engulfed the world.

**9.** Many older residents of Paris can still recall the day in 1944 when Allied troops _____ the city from German occupation.

**10.** Even fans sitting high in the stands could hear the _____ when the big fullback crashed into the line!

**11.** When they realized that sweet talk and flattery were getting them nowhere, they tried to _____ me into doing what they wanted.

**12.** We can hold down the cost of the new car we want to buy by not ordering _____ features, such as air-conditioning.

**13.** As a young and inexperienced employee, you cannot expect to hold more than a(n) _____ job in that big company.

**14.** Every eye was on us as we _____ down Main Street in our new outfits.

**15.** Next year, when we have a stronger, more experienced team, we hope to _____ the crushing defeat we have just suffered.

**16.** The impact of the head-on collision was so severe that the drivers of both vehicles were killed _____ .

**17.** Many people say that they become quite _____ when they look down from the top of a tall building.

**18.** After the heavy meal, we felt so _____ that we just sat in the living room and watched whatever was on television.

**19.** Uncle Eddie, with his _____ figure, is often called on to play Santa Claus.

**20.** Our "truth in advertising" laws are designed to discourage manufacturers from _____ the virtues of their products.

---

**Synonyms**    *Choose the word from this unit that is most nearly **the same** in meaning as each of the following groups of expressions. Write the word on the line given.*

**1.** to stroll, ramble, amble, promenade          _____

**2.** changeable, shifting, fluctuating          _____

**3.** secondary, lower; an assistant, helper          _____

**4.** the brink, edge; to approach          _____

**5.** a flood; to swamp; inundate          _____

**6.** total, out-and-out; utterly, instantly _____

**7.** to frighten, bully, browbeat, hector _____

**8.** to free, untie, unshackle, release _____

**9.** round, plump, chubby, portly; sonorous _____

**10.** a collision, blow; the shock, effect _____

**11.** a date, appointment, assignation; to meet _____

**12.** to yield, deliver up, surrender, transfer _____

**13.** a shade, hue, tone; to dye, color, stain _____

**14.** voluntary, elective, discretionary _____

**15.** lazy, unhurried, lethargic, leisurely _____

**16.** light-headed, faint; frivolous, flighty _____

**17.** reasonable, rational, sensible _____

**18.** to retaliate, get even for, settle a score _____

**19.** judgment, prudence, tact, discrimination _____

**20.** to distort, falsify, twist, exaggerate _____

---

**Antonyms**   *Choose the word from this unit that is most nearly* **opposite** *in meaning to each of the following groups of expressions. Write the word on the line given.*

**1.** absurd, ridiculous, unsound, preposterous _____

**2.** thin, angular, lean, lanky, skinny, gaunt _____

**3.** a trickle, dribble _____

**4.** constant, unchanging, steady _____

**5.** active, energetic, lively; rapid, brisk _____

**6.** to imprison, fetter, shackle, bind _____

**7.** superior, higher; a chief, supervisor _____

**8.** levelheaded, serious, earnest, sober _____

**9.** required, mandatory, compulsory _____

**10.** to speed, race, hurry, dash, scurry, rush _____

**11.** to bleach, whiten _____

**12.** partial, incomplete; by degrees _____

**Choosing the Right Word**  *Encircle the **boldface** word that more satisfactorily completes each of the following sentences.*

1. A fastball pitcher will often try to (**intimidate, tint**) an opposing batter by "shaving" him with an inside pitch.

2. It is sad to see how, in just a few years, the lean young athlete has allowed himself to become flabby and (**giddy, rotund**).

3. Many people, unhappy with what nature has given them, seek to improve their appearance by (**tinting, ceding**) their hair.

4. Letters of protest (**deluged, tinted**) the Mayor's office when he proposed an increase in the sales tax.

5. It is good for you to "stand up for your rights," but you should not do so in a way that (**verges, cedes**) on discourtesy.

6. There are times in life when you should be guided more by your feelings, without trying to be strictly (**sluggish, logical**) about everything.

7. The aged millionaire, wishing to spend his last years in peace and quiet, (**ceded, misrepresented**) all his business interests to his sons.

8. In times of crisis, we may be called on to (**deluge, subordinate**) our personal interests to the needs of the nation as a whole.

9. He soon learned that the moods of a youngster — happy one moment, miserable the next — can be as (**variable, sluggish**) as the winds.

10. Many Western films include a character who is out to (**intimidate, avenge**) a wrong done to a close friend or relative.

11. Modern household appliances have done much to (**liberate, deluge**) homemakers from tedious and time-consuming chores.

12. The invitation to the party said that formal wear was (**optional, sluggish**).

13. I look forward to the time when my parents will agree that I have reached the "age of (**discretion, misrepresentation**)."

14. I plan to write a term paper that will discuss the different ways in which television has had a major (**impact, verge**) on American life.

15. If you know that you are late for school, why do you (**saunter, verge**) along as though you had all the time in the world?

16. We held a meeting to discuss why the sale of tickets to the class dance has been so (**sluggish, rotund**) and what we can do about it.

17. Only the (**sluggish, outright**) repeal of this unfair nuisance tax will satisfy the voters.

18. This biased editorial has deliberately (**misrepresented, intimidated**) the stand of our candidate on the important issues of the election.

19. We had regarded her as a rather (**rotund, giddy**) young girl, but in this tough situation she showed that she had courage and good sense.

20. At the State Fair, we separated to visit different exhibits, but we agreed to (**saunter, rendezvous**) at the refreshment stand at five o'clock.

**Analogies**  *In each of the following, encircle the item that best completes the comparison*

**1. pirate** is to **booty** as
a. banker is to check
b. thief is to loot
c. customer is to store
d. judge is to profit

**2. rotund** is to **shape** as
a. tiny is to size
b. wide is to length
c. wet is to volume
d. orange is to capacity

**3. gullible** is to **deceive** as
a. taut is to stretch
b. sluggish is to move
c. jovial is to surprise
d. crotchety is to annoy

**4. sluggish** is to **speed** as
a. nimble is to skill
b. logical is to reason
c. giddy is to seriousness
d. optional is to meaning

**5. affluence** is to **wealthy** as
a. poverty is to penniless
b. knowledge is to ignorant
c. talent is to average
d. power is to political

**6. pathetic** is to **pity** as
a. subordinate is to concern
b. outright is to joy
c. illicit is to laughter
d. sinister is to fear

**7. immobile** is to **move** as
a. impossible is to touch
b. impassable is to cross
c. important is to see
d. improper is to do

**8. martial** is to **war** as
a. legal is to government
b. moral is to crime
c. financial is to money
d. judicial is to religion

**9. fatality** is to **dead** as
a. onset is to tired
b. format is to dirty
c. injury is to hurt
d. memorandum is to hungry

**10. diplomat** is to **discretion** as
a. showoff is to modesty
b. daredevil is to cowardice
c. hothead is to rashness
d. spoilsport is to enthusiasm

**11. bully** is to **intimidate** as
a. coward is to avenge
b. swindler is to cheat
c. judge is to retrieve
d. patient is to dissect

**12. immerse** is to **liquid** as
a. hide is to air
b. bury is to ground
c. freeze is to fire
d. illuminate is to cold

**13. perishable** is to **spoil** as
a. fragile is to break
b. optional is to use
c. immobile is to shift
d. inflammatory is to extinguish

**14. dribble** is to **deluge** as
a. invention is to innovation
b. dye is to tint
c. spray is to cascade
d. format is to design

**15. liar** is to **prevaricate** as
a. showoff is to hide
b. pickpocket is to steal
c. spoilsport is to amuse
d. culprit is to rescue

**16. prisoner** is to **manacle** as
a. dancer is to tie
b. nurse is to helmet
c. king is to crown
d. farmer is to tuxedo

**17. slavery** is to **liberate** as
a. trap is to release
b. problem is to create
c. accident is to observe
d. injury is to suffer

**18. snake** is to **writhe** as
a. lion is to cringe
b. leopard is to saunter
c. butterfly is to intimidate
d. snail is to dawdle

**19. variable** is to **change** as
a. perishable is to decay
b. minimum is to time
c. outright is to disease
d. illicit is to aging

**20. relish** is to **hot dog** as
a. straw is to soda
b. cherry is to sundae
c. bun is to hamburger
d. cup is to coffee

---

**Definitions**     *In each of the following groups, encircle the word or expression that means the same as the word in boldface type in the introductory phrase.*

**1.** enjoyed the **martial** music
a. slow          b. military          c. operatic          d. popular

**2.** performed **illicit** acts
a. illegal          b. charitable          c. honorable          d. lively

**3.** will not allow ourselves to be **intimidated**
a. cheated          b. amused          c. hurt          d. bullied

**4. quash** a revolt
a. put down          b. publicize          c. report          d. start

**5.** the **format** of the TV program
a. popularity          b. layout          c. length          d. value

**6.** a person of **affluence**
a. wealth          b. knowledge          c. wisdom          d. experience

**7.** showed outstanding **discretion**
a. unselfishness          b. judgment          c. treachery          d. courage

**8.** the **impact** of the new factory
a. advertising          b. pollution          c. needs          d. effect

**9. avenge** a wrong
a. explain          b. get even for          c. hide          d. apologize for

**10.** laden with **booty**
a. cares          b. baggage          c. bills          d. loot

**11. authorize** the necessary funds
a. approve          b. collect          c. spend          d. determine

**12. scoured** the attic
a. burned down          b. searched          c. messed up          d. avoided

**13. partition** the country
a. conquer          b. free          c. divide          d. study

**14.** a highway **fatality**
a. patrol          b. accident          c. robber          d. death

**15. manacle** the suspect
a. release          b. handcuff          c. try          d. capture

**16.** read the **memorandum**
a. newspaper          b. speech          c. report          d. novel

**17.** an **impassable** country road
a. beautiful          b. winding          c. bumpy          d. blocked

**Shades of Meaning**

*Read each sentence carefully. Then encircle the item that best completes the statement below the sentence.*

Over the years countless students have recited the rotund lines of Edgar Allan Poe's famous poem "The Raven." **(2)**

**1.** The word **rotund** in line 1 most nearly means
a. plump     b. stout     c. round     d. sonorous

Our teacher wrote "x + 9" on the board to give an example of a mathematical expression containing a variable. **(2)**

**2.** In line 2 the word **variable** is best defined as
a. difficult problem     c. unknown value
b. mistake     d. solution

Not only was Abraham Lincoln a master of English prose, but by all accounts he possessed a keen sense of humor and relished a good story. **(2)**

**3.** The word **relished** in line 2 is used to mean
a. enjoyed     b. told     c. collected     d. concocted

With the death of Stonewall Jackson in May of 1863, Confederate commander Robert E. Lee lost his ablest subordinate. **(2)**

**4.** In line 2 the word **subordinate** is best defined as
a. adviser     b. strategist     c. ally     d. lieutenant

By the time of Lee's surrender at Appomattox in April 1865 the war-making capacity of the South had been destroyed outright. **(2)**

**5.** The word **outright** in line 2 most nearly means
a. instantly     b. completely     c. gradually     d. partially

---

**Antonyms**

*In each of the following groups, encircle the word or expression that is most nearly **opposite** in meaning to the word in **boldface type** in the introductory phrase.*

**1.** encouraged us to **persevere**
a. cheat     b. give up     c. reply     d. answer

**2.** a very **gullible** person
a. rich     b. silly     c. tall     d. suspicious

**3.** **liberate** the country
a. enslave     b. study     c. rule     d. visit

**4.** an **optional** course
a. new     b. interesting     c. required     d. difficult

**5.** the **minimum** amount allowed by law
a. only     b. latest     c. usual     d. greatest

**6.** a **taut** line
a. slack     b. frayed     c. sturdy     d. new

**7.** **expend** energy
a. use     b. lack     c. conserve     d. require

**8.** a truly **pathetic** sight
a. amusing         b. unusual         c. ordinary         d. sad

**9.** in a **jovial** mood
a. puzzling        b. gloomy          c. talkative        d. merry

**10.** his **rotund** figure in the doorway
a. round           b. dark            c. frightening      d. lanky

**11. perishable** goods
a. foreign         b. expensive       c. colorful         d. durable

**12. relish** the idea
a. consider        b. loathe          c. examine          d. invent

**13.** a **deluge** of letters
a. trickle         b. receiver        c. writer           d. flood

**14.** became **sluggish** after lunch
a. talkative       b. friendly        c. active           d. sleepy

**15.** my **crotchety** boss
a. new             b. agreeable       c. former           d. overworked

---

**Completing the Sentence**

*From the following lists of words, choose the one that best completes each of the sentences below. Write the word in the space provided.*

### Group A

| | | | |
|---|---|---|---|
| **scour** | **impact** | **minimum** | **reminisce** |
| **rendezvous** | **writhe** | **nimble** | **saunter** |

**1.** How dare you _____ into the classroom more than twenty minutes after the ringing of the late bell!

**2.** I envy Lenore because she seems to be able to accomplish whatever she wishes with a(n) _____ of effort.

**3.** The three groups of backpackers will _____ at the south end of Memorial Bridge at 7:00 A.M.

**4.** I _____ in embarrassment whenever they start to boast about their family's wealth.

**5.** It may be fun to _____ about the past, but isn't it more important to do something about the future?

### Group B

| | | | |
|---|---|---|---|
| **deluge** | **booty** | **scour** | **arrears** |
| **authorize** | **verge** | **dissect** | **manacle** |

**1.** If you are so deeply in _____ on the payments for your hi-fi equipment, how can you even think of buying a motorbike?

2. We are going to _____ the fire-drill procedure until we find out why it works so poorly.

3. Who _____ you to use the school's duplicating machine for your own purposes?

4. After riding with him, I am prepared to say that his way of driving a car _____ on the hair-raising.

5. Since there is not the slightest chance that the prisoners will offer any resistance or try to escape, I don't see why you feel that it is necessary to _____ them.

## Word Families

**A.** *On the line provided, write a **noun form** of each of the following words.*

EXAMPLE: intimidate — **intimidation**

1. authorize      _____
2. dissect      _____
3. expend      _____
4. gullible      _____
5. immerse      _____
6. pathetic      _____
7. persevere      _____
8. prevaricate      _____
9. reminisce      _____
10. liberate      _____
11. jovial      _____
12. nimble      _____
13. optional      _____
14. retrieve      _____
15. variable      _____

**B.** *On the line provided, write an **adjective** related to each of the following words.*

EXAMPLE: avenge — **vengeful**

1. fatality      _____
2. affluence      _____
3. discretion      _____
4. reminisce      _____
5. innovation      _____

**C.** *On the line provided, write a **verb** related to each of the following words.*

EXAMPLE: inflammatory — **inflame**

**1.** minimum _____

**2.** perishable _____

**3.** variable _____

**4.** innovation _____

**5.** gullible _____

**6.** immobile _____

---

**Filling
the Blanks**

*Encircle the pair of words that best complete each of the following passages.*

**1.** Joan of Arc spent most of her brief career as the "warrior maiden of France" attempting to _____ lands that the French had been forced to _____ to England as a result of English victories in the initial stages of the Hundred Years' War.

   a. partition . . . expend         c. liberate . . . misrepresent
   b. avenge . . . authorize        d. retrieve . . . cede

**2.** The _____ of their sudden collision left one of the players _____ on the ice in agony, while the other was hurled five feet into the air.

   a. format . . . cringing          c. fatality . . . verging
   b. impact . . . writhing         d. onset . . . scouring

**3.** During "Operation Dragnet," the police _____ the entire city in search of the two _____ who had pulled off the daring bank robbery.

   a. immersed . . . fatalities      c. scoured . . . culprits
   b. quashed . . . innovators     d. deluged . . . subordinates

**4.** The bully down the block is so big and so _____ that I find myself unconsciously _____ in fear every time he looks in my direction.

   a. intimidating . . . cringing     c. sinister . . . dawdling
   b. rotund . . . prevaricating     d. martial . . . sauntering

**5.** The Emancipation Proclamation _____ Southern blacks once and for all from the _____ that bound them to a life of servitude and humiliation.

   a. immersed . . . arrears        c. subordinated . . . memoranda
   b. liberated . . . manacles      d. retrieved . . . tints

**Analogies**　*In each of the following, encircle the item that best completes the comparison.*

**1. nimble** is to **agility** as
a. immobile is to liveliness
b. gross is to sensitivity
c. arid is to variety
d. limber is to flexibility

**2. jovial** is to **merriment** as
a. sage is to joy
b. serene is to bliss
c. martial is to peace
d. sinister is to contentment

**3. highwayman** is to **waylay** as
a. assailant is to assault
b. inhabitant is to manipulate
c. culprit is to idolize
d. oaf is to forsake

**4. synopsis** is to **compress** as
a. memorandum is to discredit
b. ovation is to depict
c. commentary is to dissect
d. dispatch is to reimburse

**5. maximum** is to **minimum** as
a. immense is to petty
b. giddy is to eerie
c. pathetic is to pitiful
d. disinterested is to impartial

**6. apparel** is to **wear** as
a. equipment is to read
b. entertainment is to live
c. food is to eat
d. furniture is to break

**7. manacle** is to **constrain** as
a. spur is to motivate
b. leash is to liberate
c. chain is to generate
d. handcuff is to designate

**8. crotchety** is to **amiable** as
a. famished is to ravenous
b. mortal is to perishable
c. immediate is to instantaneous
d. sluggish is to energetic

**9. taut** is to **leeway** as
a. variable is to change
b. cramped is to elbowroom
c. global is to area
d. optional is to choice

**10. setback** is to **discourage** as
a. victory is to delight
b. loss is to please
c. triumph is to sadden
d. defeat is to thrill

---

**Shades of Meaning**　*Read each sentence carefully. Then encircle the item that best completes the statement below the sentence.*

A brief scan of the rugged terrain that lay ahead was enough to tell us that a long, difficult hike was in store. (2)

**1.** In line 1 the word **scan** most nearly means
a. exploration　b. examination　c. discussion　d. mapping

Instructing an actor how to play a part, Prince Hamlet advises, "Let your own discretion be your tutor." (2)

**2.** The word **discretion** in line 2 is used to mean
a. judgment　b. freedom　c. choice　d. talent

Tacitus tells us in *The Annals* that Emperor Nero ordered the dispatch of scores of his enemies—both real and imagined. (2)

**3.** In line 1 the word **dispatch** is best defined as
a. promptness　b. communication　c. execution　d. conviction

Among those who perished at Nero's bidding was the philosopher and dramatist Lucius Annaeus Seneca, who had been the emperor's tutor. **(2)**

**4.** The word **perished** in line 1 most nearly means
- a. profited
- b. informed on others
- c. died
- d. were exiled

No visit to Paris is complete without a saunter down its most famous boulevard, the Champs-Élysées. **(2)**

**5.** In line 1 the word **saunter** is best defined as
- a. scamper
- b. stroll
- c. race
- d. hike

---

**Filling the Blanks** — *Encircle the pair of words that best complete each of the following passages.*

**1.** When the volcano erupted, huge quantities of molten lava and boiling mud _____ like some fiery waterfall down the steep sides of the mountain, _____ the region round about.
- a. cascaded . . . devastating
- b. deluged . . . befuddling
- c. billowed . . . vacating
- d. writhed . . . stranding

**2.** Though many of the hardships that the peoples of the world face today are purely local, the _____ of those suffering from hunger and malnutrition is of truly _____ proportions.
- a. enigma . . . incomprehensible
- b. queue . . . adverse
- c. plight . . . global
- d. maze . . . acute

**3.** "Despite all the problems and _____ we have experienced in recent months, we must _____ in our endeavor to achieve the goals we have set for the company this year," I said.
- a. revocations . . . verge
- b. setbacks . . . persevere
- c. keepsakes . . . cringe
- d. vocations . . . tarry

**4.** Though surrounded on all sides by superior forces, the inhabitants of the _____ city were able to keep the enemy at bay for a long time by maintaining a steady _____ of missiles from their walls and towers.
- a. encompassed . . . rendezvous
- b. partitioned . . . repast
- c. restricted . . . oracle
- d. besieged . . . barrage

**5.** During the lengthy dry spell that the area experiences every summer, the vegetation _____ completely away, and the landscape takes on a surprising resemblance to the kind of _____ found on the moon.
- a. frays . . . format
- b. withers . . . terrain
- c. blusters . . . booty
- d. cedes . . . duration

# Unit 10

**Definitions**

*Note carefully the spelling, pronunciation, and definition of each of the following words. Then write the word in the blank space in the illustrative phrase following.*

**1. abominable**
(ə 'bäm ə nə bəl)

(*adj.*) arousing hatred; disgusting, detestable

an _____ idea

**2. bumbling**
('bəm bliŋ)

(*adj.*) blundering and awkward; (*n.*) clumsiness

a _____ approach to a problem

**3. consequence**
('kän sə kwens)

(*n.*) a result, effect; importance

accept the _____ of one's actions

**4. delude**
(di 'lüd)

(*v.*) to fool, deceive; to mislead utterly

only _____ himself

**5. dole**
(dōl)

(*v.*) to give out in small amounts; (*n.*) money, food, or other necessities given as charity; a small portion

_____ out the last of the food

**6. engulf**
(en 'gəlf)

(*v.*) to swallow up, overwhelm

_____ in flames

**7. foil**
(foil)

(*v.*) to defeat, to keep from gaining some end; (*n.*) a thin sheet of metal; a light fencing sword; a person or thing serving as a contrast to another

_____ the treacherous plot

**8. formulate**
('fôr myə lāt)

(*v.*) to express definitely or systematically; to devise, invent; to state as a formula

_____ a new energy policy

**9. initiative**
(i 'nish ə tiv)

(*n.*) the taking of the first step or move; the ability to act without being directed or urged from the outside

on our own _____

**10. memento**
(mə 'men tō)

(*n.*) something that serves as a reminder

a _____ of our trip

**11. nonconformist**
(nän kən 'fôr mist)

(*n.*) a person who refuses to follow established ideas or ways of doing things; (*adj.*) of or relating to the unconventional

a _____ with a mind of his own

**12. null and void**
(nəl and void)

(*adj.*) without legal force or effect; no longer binding

a treaty that has become _____

**13. panorama**
(pan ə 'ram ə)

(*n.*) a wide, unobstructed view of an area; a complete survey of a subject; a continuously passing or changing scene; range or spectrum

the _____ of American history

78

**14. posterity**
(pä 'ster ət ē)

(*n.*) all of a person's offspring, descendants; all future generations

for the benefit of _____

**15. pry**
(prī)

(*v.*) to pull loose by force; to look at closely or inquisitively; to be nosy about something

_____ the lid off

**16. refurbish**
(ri 'fər bish)

(*v.*) to brighten, freshen, or polish; to restore or improve

_____ her wardrobe

**17. resourceful**
(ri 'sôrs fəl)

(*adj.*) able to deal promptly and effectively with all sorts of problems; clever in finding ways and means of getting along

a _____ leader

**18. rigorous**
('rig ər əs)

(*adj.*) severe, harsh, strict; thoroughly logical

a _____ judge

**19. subsequent**
('səb sə kwənt)

(*adj.*) coming after; following in time, place, or order

_____ developments

**20. unerring**
(ən 'ər iŋ)

(*adj.*) making no mistakes, faultless, completely accurate

_____ judgment

---

**Completing the Sentence**

*Choose the word from this unit that best completes each of the following sentences. Write it in the space given.*

1. Many an artist whose work has been overlooked in his or her own lifetime has had to trust to _____ for appreciation.

2. The term "_____" was first applied in the 1660s to English Protestants who dissented from the Church of England.

3. The first meeting will be in the school auditorium, but all _____ meetings will be held in the homes of our members.

4. What a disappointment to hear that dull and _____ speech when we were expecting a clear, forceful, and interesting statement!

5. Professional baseball players get themselves into shape for the upcoming season by undergoing a _____ training period each spring.

6. You may think that the crude way he has behaved is slightly amusing, but I think it is _____ and inexcusable.

7. All that you will need to _____ that dilapidated old house is lots of time, lots of skill, lots of enthusiasm, and lots of money.

8. These old photographs may not look like much, but I treasure them as a(n) _____ of the last summer my entire family spent together.

**10**

9. At the time it occurred, that mistake didn't seem to be too important, but it had _____ that have hurt me down to the present day.

10. From the observation deck of the World Trade Center one may enjoy a sweeping _____ of New York Harbor.

11. The alert employee _____ an attempted robbery by setting off the alarm promptly.

12. As a tennis player, Sue doesn't have much speed or power, but she hits the ball with _____ accuracy.

13. We must _____ a detailed response that leaves no doubt about our position on this important issue.

14. A truly _____ administrator always seems to be able to find an effective way of dealing with any problem that may come up.

15. Anyone who _____ into someone else's business runs the risk of opening a can of worms.

16. Huge clouds of smoke and ash from the angry volcano _____ the sleepy little villages that nestled on its flanks.

17. Since I was able to prove in court that the salesperson had lied to me, the contract I had signed was declared _____.

18. During World War II, food became so scarce in Great Britain that the government _____ it out to consumers in very small amounts.

19. Rather than sit back and wait for the enemy to attack him, the general took the _____ and delivered the first blow.

20. Like so many other young people, he has been _____ into the false belief that there is an easy way to success.

---

**Synonyms**    Choose the word from this unit that is most nearly **the same** in meaning as each of the following groups of expressions. Write the word on the line given.

1. canceled, invalid, repealed, abolished _____

2. a maverick, individualist, bohemian _____

3. following, next, succeeding, ensuing _____

4. inventive, ingenious, skillful _____

5. tough, trying, challenging, stringent _____

6. to express, articulate; to invent _____

**7.** a view, vista; an overview, survey  _____

**8.** the first step; leadership, enterprise  _____

**9.** a remembrance, keepsake, souvenir, token  _____

**10.** to frustrate, thwart, counter; a rapier  _____

**11.** sure, certain, unfailing, faultless  _____

**12.** to remodel, renew, improve, spruce up  _____

**13.** disgusting, hateful, despicable, loathsome  _____

**14.** to swallow up, overwhelm, consume  _____

**15.** a handout; to ration, allot, distribute  _____

**16.** to snoop, meddle  _____

**17.** a result, outcome; significance  _____

**18.** to trick, fool, mislead, deceive, hoodwink  _____

**19.** blundering, clumsy, stumbling  _____

**20.** offspring, descendants; future generations  _____

---

**Antonyms**     *Choose the word from this unit that is most nearly*
***opposite** in meaning to each of the following groups of
expressions. Write the word on the line given.*

**1.** in effect, binding, valid  _____

**2.** easy, lax, indulgent, undemanding  _____

**3.** to dilapidate, run down  _____

**4.** previous, prior, preceding  _____

**5.** faulty, fallible, unreliable  _____

**6.** uninventive, incompetent, dull-witted  _____

**7.** forceful, effective, skillful, adroit  _____

**8.** a cause, source  _____

**9.** to aid, abet, assist, advance, promote  _____

**10.** praiseworthy, delightful, charming  _____

**11.** laziness, sloth, shiftlessness  _____

**12.** to mind one's own business  _____

**13.** ancestry; ancestors, forebears; the past  _____

**Choosing the Right Word**

*Encircle the **boldface** word that more satisfactorily completes each of the following sentences.*

1. All these things in the attic may seem like a lot of junk to you, but to me they are priceless (**mementos, foils**) of childhood.

2. In devising the Constitution, the Founding Fathers sought to "secure the blessings of liberty to ourselves and our (**posterity, foils**)."

3. The war that began with Germany's invasion of Poland in 1939 spread until it had (**pried, engulfed**) almost the entire world.

4. One of the signs of a truly democratic nation is that it gives protection and freedom to (**initiatives, nonconformists**) who espouse unpopular views.

5. We all know that it is a long time since the speeding laws in our community have been (**subsequently, rigorously**) enforced.

6. By coaxing and questioning hour after hour, Tom finally managed to (**pry, delude**) the big secret from his sister.

7. He may look like a very ordinary little man, but he is in fact a figure of real (**memento, consequence**) in the state government.

8. Here I am on my first vacation in three years, and I have to put up with this (**abominable, bumbling**) weather day after day!

9. She hopes to win the election by convincing voters that the city's troubles result from the (**bumbling, unerring**) policies of the present Mayor.

10. What we lightly refer to as our "foreign policy" in fact embraces a vast (**panorama, memento**) of aims and objectives, problems and concerns.

11. With his serious face and his dignified way of speaking, he is an excellent (**foil, memento**) for the clownish comedian.

12. Perhaps he doesn't seem to be very bright, but he has a(n) (**rigorous, unerring**) instinct for anything that may make money for him.

13. It is too late to attempt to (**refurbish, delude**) the old city charter; we must have a completely new plan for our city government.

14. "We must (**engulf, formulate**) a plan to deal with this new situation and carry it out as quickly as possible," the President said.

15. Do you think the United States should take the (**initiative, dole**) in trying to bring about a compromise peace in the Middle East?

16. Since you have failed to carry out your promises, I must tell you that the agreement between us is now (**unerring, null and void**).

17. If you think that you can get away with selling overpriced products to the people of this town, you are (**deluding, refurbishing**) yourself.

18. The lawyer made the point that her client had been at the scene of the crime before the murder but not (**subsequent, rigorous**) to it.

19. Why is it that such hardworking, self-reliant people now have to depend on a (**foil, dole**) of food and other necessities from charitable agencies?

20. Brad is the kind of (**rigorous, resourceful**) quarterback who can always come up with something new when it is a matter of victory or defeat.

# Unit 11

**Definitions**

**1. alias**
('ā lē əs)

(*n.*) an assumed name, especially as used to hide one's identity; (*adj.*) otherwise called

went by the _____ of Smith

**2. amble**
('am bəl)

(*v.*) to walk slowly, stroll; (*n.*) an easy pace; a leisurely walk

_____ through the park

**3. burly**
('bər lē)

(*adj.*) big and strong; muscular

as _____ as a lumberjack

**4. distort**
(dis 'tôrt)

(*v.*) to give a false or misleading account of; to twist out of shape

_____ the facts

**5. dogged**
('dôg əd)

(*adj.*) persistent, stubbornly determined, refusing to give up

fought with _____ courage

**6. dumfounded**
('dəm faůnd əd)

(*adj.*) so amazed that one is unable to speak; bewildered

_____ by the development

**7. extinct**
(ek 'stiŋkt)

(*adj.*) no longer in existence; gone out of use

an _____ language

**8. fossil**
('fäs əl)

(*n.*) the remains or traces of an animal or plant that lived in the past; an extremely old-fashioned person or thing; (*adj.*) having qualities that belong to the remote past

rocks bearing _____

**9. grit**
(grit)

(*n.*) very fine sand or gravel; courage in the face of hardship or danger; (*v.*) to grind; to make a grating sound

some _____ in the gas line

**10. inevitable**
(in 'ev ə tə bəl)

(*adj.*) sure to happen, unavoidable

the _____ ending

**11. ingrained**
(in 'grānd)

(*adj.*) fixed deeply and firmly; worked into the grain or fiber; forming a part of the inmost being

an _____ habit

**12. meteoric**
(mē tē 'ôr ik)

(*adj.*) resembling a meteor in speed; having sudden and temporary brilliance similar to a meteor's

a _____ rise to fame

**13. parody**
('par o dē)

(*n*) a humorous or ridiculous imitation; (*v.*) to make fun of something by imitating it

a clever _____ of the novel

**14. prevail**
(pri 'vāl)

(*v.*) to triumph over; succeed; to exist widely, be in general use; to get someone to do something by urging

_____ against all obstacles

**15. rend**
(rend)

(*v.*) to tear to pieces; split violently apart (*past tense*, rent)

an issue that _____ public opinion

**16. replenish**
(ri 'plen ish)

(*v.*) to fill again, make good, replace

_____ our supplies

**17. rummage**
('rəm əj)

(*v.*) to search through, investigate the contents of; (*n.*) an active search; a collection of odd items

_____ around in the basement

**18. skimp**
(skimp)

(*v.*) to save, be thrifty; to be extremely sparing with; to give little attention or effort to

_____ on food

**19. sleuth**
(slüth)

(*n.*) a detective

a famous _____

**20. vandalism**
('van dəl iz əm)

(*n.*) deliberate and pointless destruction of public or private property

pass laws against _____

---

**Completing
the Sentence**

*Choose the word from this unit that best completes each of the following sentences. Write it in the space given.*

**1.** The rock singer enjoyed a sudden, _____ rise in popularity, but his career faded just as quickly as it had blossomed.

**2.** There is an old saying that nothing is really _____ except death and taxes.

**3.** Isn't it a shame that our School Board must spend thousands of dollars every year just to repair the damage caused by _____ .

**4.** We saw a bolt of lightning _____ a huge limb from the mighty oak tree.

**5.** The grime on the mechanic's hands was so deeply _____ that even a thorough scrubbing couldn't entirely remove it.

**6.** We greatly admired the _____ determination and patience that the disabled veteran showed in learning to master a wheelchair.

**7.** In the late 19th century, Sir Arthur Conan Doyle created one of the most famous _____ in literature, Sherlock Holmes.

**8.** Her ability to _____ the words and gestures of prominent Americans makes her an excellent comic impressionist.

**9.** If you truly want to improve your math grades, you should not continue to _____ so often on your homework.

**10.** We were nothing less than _____ when we saw the immense damage that the hurricane had done in so brief a time.

**11.** Whenever our team needs a few yards to make a first down, we call on our big, _____ fullback to crash through the line.

**12.** Since coal was formed from the decayed bodies of plants that lived many millions of years ago, it is considered a kind of _____ fuel.

**13.** The cruise ship stopped at the port both to give the passengers a chance to go ashore and to _____ the water supply.

**14.** The old custom of celebrating the Fourth of July with a fireworks display still _____ in many American towns.

**15.** Even though so many people were criticizing and ridiculing him, he had the _____ to continue doing what he felt was right.

**16.** The old con artist had used so many _____ over the course of his criminal career that he sometimes forgot his real name!

**17.** Her face was so _____ with pain and suffering that at first I did not recognize her.

**18.** Isn't it fun on a rainy day to _____ about in the attic and look for interesting odds and ends?

**19.** As the buffalo began to decrease sharply in numbers, conservationists feared that it might become totally _____ .

**20.** After our furious gallop across the countryside, we allowed our tired horses to _____ back to the stable.

---

**Synonyms**    *Choose the word from this unit that is most nearly **the same** in meaning as each of the following groups of expressions. Write the word on the line given.*

**1.** deep-seated, fixed, deep-rooted, indelible       _____

**2.** to disfigure, misshape; to falsify       _____

**3.** a satire, travesty; to lampoon, burlesque       _____

**4.** to refill, restock, refresh, restore       _____

**5.** brilliant, blazing

**6.** unavoidable, inescapable, fated

**7.** to rule, reign; to overcome, conquor

**8.** to split, cleave, splinter, tear asunder

**9.** strapping, hefty, beefy, brawny

**10.** to be stingy; to scrimp, cut corners

**11.** determined, untiring, persistent

**12.** dirt, sand; courage, mettle; to grind

**13.** to delve into, sift through, poke around

**14.** speechless, stunned, flabbergasted

**15.** petrified remains; a relic

**16.** died out, vanished

**17.** a detective, investigator, gumshoe

**18.** to stroll, saunter; a walk, ramble

**19.** willful destruction, malicious defacement

**20.** an assumed name, pseudonym

---

**Antonyms**    *Choose the word from this unit that is most nearly **opposite** in meaning to each of the following groups of expressions. Write the word on the line given.*

**1.** avoidable, escapable, preventable

**2.** one's real name, given name, legal name

**3.** to empty, drain, deplete, sap

**4.** still alive, surviving, extant

**5.** weak, puny, delicate, frail

**6.** slow, sluggish, gradual

**7.** to be defeated, go under, succumb

**8.** to gallop, dash, sprint, run, race, rush

**9.** wishy-washy, faltering, irresolute

**10.** timidity, cowardice, faintheartedness

**11.** superficial, shallow, skin-deep

**12.** to be extravagant, splurge, lavish

**Choosing the**  *Encircle the **boldface** word that more satisfactorily*
**Right Word**  *completes each of the following sentences.*

1. The prejudices of a bigot are sometimes so (**Ingrained, dumfounded**) that it is very difficult to get rid of them.

2. Although it is sometimes hard, we must have faith that in the long run justice and decency will (**skimp, prevail**).

3. The defenders of the Alamo put up such a (**burly, dogged**) resistance that the enemy had a hard time taking the place.

4. I am exhausted now, but all I need is a satisfying meal, a hot shower, and a good night's sleep to (**replenish, rend**) my energies.

5. The aging actor trying to play the part of a young man seemed no more than a (**sleuth, parody**) of the great performer he once was.

6. Visiting the school I had attended so many years before made me feel like a creature from the far past—a living (**rummage, fossil**).

7. Isn't it foolish to think that just because of his (**meteoric, burly**) physique he has no interest in art or music?

8. I hope to pick up some real bargains at the (**rummage, rend**) sale being held in our civic center.

9. It may be, as you say, that this volcano has been (**extinct, dumfounded**) for many years, but isn't there some danger that it may come to life again?

10. Whether the window was broken accidentally or as an act of (**parody, vandalism**), the fact remains that it is broken and must be paid for.

11. Is there anything more romantic than a nighttime (**amble, parody**) upon the moonlit decks of a mighty ocean liner?

12. To avoid a lot of unwanted attention, the famous rock star registered in the hotel under a(n) (**sleuth, alias**).

13. Suddenly, the stillness of the early morning hours was (**rent, rummaged**) by a single shot!

14. "I'll have two franks with all the fixings," I said to the vendor, "and don't (**prevail, skimp**) on the mustard!"

15. Since it is possible for nations to settle their disagreements in a reasonable way, we refuse to believe that war is (**inevitable, dumfounded**).

16. We scorn all those who would deliberately bend the truth and (**distort, amble**) history in order to suit the political needs of their day.

17. An art historian who is trying to verify the authenticity of a painting acts more like a (**sleuth, rummage**) than a critic.

18. I know that you don't like the idea of working in a gas station, but you'll just have to (**replenish, grit**) your teeth and do it.

19. No, I wasn't (**ingrained, dumfounded**) to be chosen the most popular member of the class, but maybe I was just a little surprised!

20. His (**dogged, meteoric**) success at such an early age left him unprepared to handle the disappointments and failures that came to him later in life.

# Unit 12

**Definitions**

*Note carefully the spelling, pronunciation, and definition of each of the following words. Then write the word in the blank space in the illustrative phrase following.*

**1. abduct**
(ab 'dəkt)

(*v.*) to kidnap, carry off by force

_____ a person for ransom

**2. ambiguous**
(am 'big yü əs)

(*adj.*) not clear; having two or more possible meanings

an _____ answer

**3. balk**
(bôk)

(*v.*) to stop short and refuse to go on; to block
(*n.*) (in baseball) an illegal motion made by a pitcher

_____ at finishing one's dinner

**4. compact**
(*v., adj.*, kəm
'pact; *n.*, 'käm
pact)

(*adj.*) closely and firmly packed together; small; (*v.*) to squeeze together; (*n.*) an agreement between parties; a small case containing a mirror and face powder; a small car

a _____ disc

**5. confer**
(kən 'fər)

(*v.*) to consult, talk over, exchange opinions; to present as a gift, favor, or honor

will _____ before taking action

**6. earmark**
('ir mark)

(*v.*) to mark an animal's ear for identification; to set aside for a special purpose; (*n.*) an identifying mark or feature

_____ a sheep

**7. frigid**
('frij id)

(*adj.*) extremely cold; lacking in warmth of feeling

a _____ climate

**8. implement**
('im plə mənt)

(*n.*) an instrument, tool; (*v.*) to put into effect

farm _____

**9. incalculable**
(in 'kal kyə lə bəl)

(*adj.*) too great to be counted; unpredictable, uncertain

cause _____ damage

**10. indisputable**
(in dis 'pyüt ə bəl)

(*adj.*) beyond question or argument, definitely true

_____ evidence

**11. intensive**
(in 'ten siv)

(*adj.*) thorough, deep; showing great effort; concentrated

an _____ effort

**12. maneuver**
(mə 'nü vər)

(*n.*) a planned movement; a skillful plan; a scheme;
(*v.*) to perform or carry out such a planned movement

troops on _____

**13. sabotage**
('sab ə täzh)

(*n.*) an action taken to destroy something or to prevent it from working properly; (*v.*) to take such destructive action

take precautions against _____

**14. scant**
('skant)

(*adj.*) not enough; barely enough; marked by a small or insufficient amount

a _____ supply of food

**15. stealthy**
('stel thē)

(*adj.*) done in a way so as not to be seen or observed; sneaky; underhanded

a _____ glance

**16. strapping**
('strap iŋ)

(*adj.*) tall, strong, and healthy

a _____ young man

**17. strident**
('strīd ənt)

(*adj.*) harsh, shrill; unpleasant sounding

_____ laughter

**18. thrive**
(thrīv)

(*v.*) to grow vigorously; to grow in wealth and possessions, prosper

a business that _____

**19. titanic**
(tī 'tan ik)

(*adj.*) of enormous size, strength, power, or scope

a _____ struggle

**20. valiant**
('val yənt)

(*adj.*) possessing or acting with bravery or boldness

_____ Knights of the Round Table

---

**Completing the Sentence**

*Choose the word from this unit that best completes each of the following sentences. Write the word in the space provided.*

**1.** The breakdown of all these machines at the same time cannot simply be a coincidence; we suspect deliberate _____ .

**2.** I was amazed to see how skillfully Irma _____ that huge car through the heavy downtown traffic.

**3.** Even mighty warships were endangered by the _____ waves that loomed like mountains above them.

**4.** Since I'm afraid of heights, I usually _____ at the idea of sitting in the first row of the topmost balcony in a theater.

**5.** Why must you always be so _____ when I want you to give me a straight yes-or-no answer?

**6.** When we saw their _____ 200-pound defensive linemen, we realized that we would have a hard time running against them.

**7.** For a person who loves to argue as much as Gene does, there is nothing that is really _____ .

**8.** The new recruits were rudely awakened from their peaceful sleep by the _____ voice of the sergeant barking commands.

**9.** The cactus is an example of a plant having natural adaptations that enable it to _____ even in a very dry climate.

**10.** The millionaire has hired special guards to make sure that his children will not be _____ .

**11.** In your training course for dental assistant, you will become familiar with many of the _____ that dentists use.

**12.** No doubt our antipollution program will be expensive, but the cost of doing nothing would be simply _____ .

**13.** Each year a portion of the school budget is _____ for the purchase of new books for the library.

**14.** When the winds begin to turn _____ in November, our thoughts turn to our warm and sunny island off the coast of Florida.

**15.** In Shakespeare's words, "Cowards die many times before their deaths; the _____ never taste of death but once."

**16.** Since the time we have to prepare for the final exams is exceedingly _____ , we had better make the best of every hour.

**17.** As the day of the big game approached, our practice sessions became more and more _____ .

**18.** I prefer the _____ edition of the dictionary because it is so much lighter and less bulky than the unabridged version.

**19.** The President will _____ well-deserved honors on the retiring ambassador.

**20.** At first the zebras did not notice the _____ movements of the lions inching their way closer to the herd.

---

**Synonyms**      *Choose the word from this unit that is most nearly **the same** in meaning as each of the following groups of expressions. Write the word on the line given.*

**1.** a move, tactic; to guide, manipulate      _____

**2.** to refuse, shy away from      _____

**3.** countless, measureless; unpredictable      _____

**4.** sturdy, husky, brawny, athletic, hefty      _____

**5.** to flourish, blossom; to prosper      _____

**6.** harsh, piercing, shrill, grating      _____

**7.** to award, bestow; to consult, deliberate      _____

**8.** inadequate, meager, skimpy, bare _____

**9.** unarguable, incontestable _____

**10.** very cold, freezing; unresponsive _____

**11.** to carry off, kidnap, snatch _____

**12.** vague, uncertain, unclear, equivocal _____

**13.** tightly packed, dense; small; to compress _____

**14.** gigantic, huge, mighty, immense _____

**15.** brave, bold, courageous, heroic, gallant _____

**16.** a tool, device, instrument, utensil _____

**17.** sneaky, sly, underhanded, furtive _____

**18.** a feature, trait, attribute; to reserve _____

**19.** to vandalize, cripple, subvert, destroy _____

**20.** thoroughgoing, concentrated, heightened _____

---

**Antonyms**　　Choose the word from this unit that is most nearly **opposite** in meaning to each of the following groups of expressions. Write the word on the line given.

**1.** hot, balmy, torrid; warm, friendly _____

**2.** measurable, countable; predictable _____

**3.** questionable, debatable, arguable _____

**4.** to withdraw, take away; to withhold, deny _____

**5.** open, direct, aboveboard, forthright _____

**6.** abundant, plentiful, profuse, excessive _____

**7.** relaxed, easygoing, laid-back _____

**8.** weak, frail, fragile, delicate, puny _____

**9.** mellow, soothing, musical, honeyed _____

**10.** obvious, plain, clear, unequivocal _____

**11.** oversize, enormous, humongous, bulky _____

**12.** tiny, miniature, diminutive, pint-size _____

**13.** to wither, die, fade; to fail _____

**14.** timid, cowardly, fainthearted, "chicken" _____

| Choosing the Right Word | Encircle the **boldface** word that more satisfactorily completes each of the following sentences. |
|---|---|

1. Creeping (**stealthily, ambiguously**) through the undorbrush, the enemy came within a few yards of the stockade before the guards saw them.

2. Though the odds were greatly against them, the brave defenders of the fort waged a (**valiant, scant**) battle against the enemy's troops.

3. When we made our appeal for funds, their response was so (**intensive, frigid**) that we realized we would have to find other ways of raising money.

4. Of all the evergreens that tower in America's forests, none can surpass the height and girth of the (**titanic, strident**) California redwoods.

5. I don't think democracy can (**balk, thrive**) in an atmosphere of racial and religious hatred.

6. After straining and sweating in the hot sun for an hour, we realized that we had pushed the stalled car a(n) (**scant, intensive**) quarter mile.

7. The future is indeed (**incalculable, indisputable**), but we must face it with faith and confidence.

8. What do you think the United States should do when its representatives are (**sabotaged, abducted**) by terrorists and held for ransom?

9. Since *presently* means both "right now" and "in the future," any statement containing it must be considered (**strident, ambiguous**).

10. As election day got closer, the tone of the candidates' political oratory got more and more (**scant, strident**).

11. When he says that his analysis of the problem is (**indisputable, valiant**), all he means is that he's not willing to listen to anyone else's ideas.

12. When their pitcher committed the (**balk, earmark**), the umpire advanced our runner from first to second base.

13. In her floor exercise, the champion gymnast performed some of the most amazing (**earmarks, maneuvers**) I have ever seen.

14. Before landing on the shore of New England, the first Pilgrim settlers signed an agreement called the "Mayflower (**Compact, Maneuver**) "

15. Because her condition was so poor after the operation, she was placed in the hospital's (**stealthy, intensive**) care unit.

16. We have worked out a good plan on paper; now we must decide how we are going to (**implement, sabotage**) it.

17. Truthfulness and sincerity are the (**earmarks, compacts**) of an honest person.

18. When a country has been overrun by a conquering army, the only way the people may have to strike back is by acts of (**ambiguity, sabotage**).

19. Although our club is run more or less democratically, we don't have the time to (**confer, abduct**) about every minor detail.

20. Why is that big, (**strapping, compact**) fellow always kicking sand into the faces of 98-pound weaklings?

# Review Units 10–12

**Analogies**    *In each of the following, encircle the item that best completes the comparison.*

**1. foil** is to **fencing** as
a. hold is to wrestling
b. play is to baseball
c. signal is to football
d. bow is to archery

**2. used up** is to **replenish** as
a. run-down is to distort
b. done in is to formulate
c. worn-out is to refurbish
d. tied up is to maneuver

**3. cold** is to **frigid** as
a. tall is to long
b. hot is to fiery
c. small is to gigantic
d. narrow is to wide

**4. compact** is to **powder** as
a. wallet is to money
b. shoe is to keys
c. pocket is to pajamas
d. suitcase is to pet

**5. incalculable** is to **count** as
a. invisible is to hear
b. inevitable is to avoid
c. indisputable is to prove
d. invaluable is to own

**6. posterity** is to **after** as
a. children are to before
b. classmates are to after
c. ancestors are to before
d. relatives are to after

**7. kidnapper** is to **abduct** as
a. burglar is to rob
b. thug is to delude
c. pirate is to lie
d. thief is to murder

**8. snoop** is to **pry** as
a. spoilsport is to amuse
b. busybody is to meddle
c. sleuth is to maneuver
d. showoff is to hide

**9. scavenger** is to **rummage** as
a. vagrant is to thrive
b. vandal is to confer
c. homebody is to amble
d. beggar is to panhandle

**10. sneak thief** is to **stealthy** as
a. maven is to strident
b. klutz is to bumbling
c. yenta is to ambiguous
d. kvetch is to extinct

**11. consequence** is to **after** as
a. cause is to before
b. initiative is to after
c. result is to before
d. origin is to after

**12. pitchfork** is to **implement** as
a. house is to furniture
b. engine is to automobile
c. door is to building
d. typewriter is to machine

**13. coward** is to **valiant** as
a. fossil is to extinct
b. pickpocket is to stealthy
c. hero is to timid
d. wrestler is to burly

**14. sheep** is to **earmark** as
a. steer is to brand
b. horse is to saddle
c. mule is to plow
d. ox is to yoke

**15. scant** is to **quantity** as
a. stealthy is to volume
b. frigid is to capacity
c. rigorous is to height
d. compact is to size

**16. dogged** is to **persistence** as
a. abominable is to knowledge
b. ingrained is to enthusiasm
c. strident is to modesty
d. resourceful is to ingenuity

**17. alias** is to **criminal** as
a. nickname is to Mike
b. stage name is to sculptor
c. pen name is to author
d. surname is to animal

**18. meteoric** is to **speed** as
a. titanic is to size
b. strapping is to shape
c. burly is to duration
d. rigorous is to position

**Definitions**   *In each of the following groups, encircle the word that is best defined or suggested by the introductory expression.*

**1.** a phony name that a con artist might use to avoid detection
a. initiative   b. consequence   c. alias   d. earmark

**2.** "This old sweater with the camp monogram reminds me of the wonderful time I had last summer."
a. panorama   b. memento   c. parody   d. foil

**3.** someone who is good at tracking down clues
a. sleuth   b. implement   c. grit   d. nonconformist

**4.** said of someone who seems to be incapable of making a mistake in a math problem
a. titanic   b. unerring   c. bumbling   d. ambiguous

**5.** what we did when our water supply began to run out
a. formulate   b. thrive   c. replenish   d. prevail

**6.** what a nosy person is likely to do
a. delude   b. balk   c. confer   d. pry

**7.** said of a person who is moving about very carefully in order to escape attention
a. stealthy   b. intensive   c. strident   d. dogged

**8.** "They claim to be our friends, but I think that they are deliberately trying to make our program fail."
a. vandalism   b. sabotage   c. rummage   d. compact

**9.** "He seems to have a gift for doing the wrong thing, at the wrong time, in the wrong way."
a. strapping   b. bumbling   c. indisputable   d. rigorous

**10.** those who come after us, especially our descendants
a. abduction   b. implement   c. distortion   d. posterity

**11.** an extinct fish found in a rock
a. rummage   b. fossil   c. alias   d. balk

**12.** so shocked and amazed that I couldn't speak
a. dumfounded   b. resourceful   c. subsequent   d. meteoric

**13.** what troops go out on to train for warfare
a. panoramas   b. parodies   c. maneuvers   d. initiatives

**14.** what one of King Arthur's knights would probably be
a. abominable   b. null and void   c. valiant   d. inevitable

**15.** an answer that is open to several interpretations
a. rend   b. ambiguous   c. indisputable   d. refurbish

**16.** what a flood would probably do
a. dole   b. skimp   c. amble   d. engulf

**17.** rightly said of a dinosaur
a. extinct   b. rigorous   c. scant   d. ingrained

**18.** how one might describe a weight lifter's build
a. burly          b. scant          c. subsequent          d. stealthy

**19.** how one might describe the grains of sand on a seashore
a. meteoric          b. abominable          c. incalculable          d. rigorous

**20.** the kind of temperatures you would experience during an Arctic winter
a. extinct          b. strident          c. burly          d. frigid

---

**Shades of Meaning**          *Read each sentence carefully. Then encircle the item that best completes the statement below the sentence.*

One of the chief aims of American foreign policy in the period following World War II was to balk Soviet attempts to "export" communism to the Third World.          (2)

**1.** In line 2 the word **balk** most nearly means
a. reverse          c. monitor
b. shy away from          d. block

It is no exaggeration to compare with canned sardines the thousands of commuters compacted in rush-hour subway cars.          (2)

**2.** The word **compacted** in line 2 is best defined as
a. fleeing work          c. squeezed together
b. making deals          d. going home

Dr. Watson is often reminded by Sherlock Holmes that his astonishing solutions stem from observation and rigorous deduction, not hunches or gut feelings.          (2)

**3.** In line 2 the word **rigorous** is used to mean
a. severe          c. harsh
b. logical          d. trying

New York City's Greenwich Village has long been a favorite destination for people whose nonconformist views set them apart from the mainstream.          (2)

**4.** The word **nonconformist** in line 2 most nearly means
a. bohemian          c. foreign
b. revolutionary          d. quaint

Rather than retire from public life as he had hoped, George Washington was prevailed upon in 1789 to accept the presidency of the United States.          (2)

**5.** The best definition for the phrase **prevailed upon** in line 2 is
a. commonly expected          c. reluctantly allowed
b. successfully urged          d. secretly ordered

Thanks to my nervous bumbling, any chance our team might have had to win the tournament went out the window.          (2)

**6.** In line 1 the word **bumbling** most nearly means
a. tumbling          c. fumbling
b. rumbling          d. mumbling

**Antonyms**   In each of the following groups, encircle the word or expression that is most nearly **opposite** in meaning to the word in **boldface type** in the introductory phrase.

**1.** if war is **inevitable**
a. costly      b. avoidable      c. desired      d. foolish

**2.** understood the **consequences** of their acts
a. aims      b. criticisms      c. causes      d. results

**3.** made the agreement **null and void**
a. meaningless      b. illegal      c. vague      d. effective

**4.** said to be a **nonconformist**
a. clever leader      b. loyal follower      c. outsider      d. hard worker

**5.** **replenished** our funds
a. used up      b. counted      c. budgeted      d. increased

**6.** a **frigid** afternoon
a. sweltering      b. icy      c. wasted      d. busy

**7.** **prevailed** in the election
a. won out      b. lost      c. took part      d. campaigned

**8.** a **strident** voice
a. loud      b. soft      c. strong      d. harsh

**9.** an **indisputable** point
a. new      b. proven      c. debatable      d. strong

**10.** a **compact** kitchen
a. efficient      b. huge      c. modern      d. costly

**11.** found their viewpoint **abominable**
a. hateful      b. strange      c. praiseworthy      d. questionable

**12.** was **dumfounded** by the news
a. astonished      b. saddened      c. amazed      d. unmoved

**13.** a very **ambiguous** reply
a. wordy      b. strange      c. clear      d. brief

**14.** a **burly** build
a. delicate      b. fat      c. tough      d. muscular

**15.** **subsequent** events
a. odd      b. prior      c. funny      d. disturbing

**16.** **scant** resources
a. scarce      b. new      c. wasted      d. plentiful

**17.** **amble** through the meadow
a. saunter      b. trudge      c. stroll      d. rush

**18.** **foil** the plan
a. assist      b. examine      c. report      d. thwart

**19.** a **thriving** plant
a. colorful      b. dying      c. poisonous      d. expensive

**20.** an **extinct** volcano
a. fossil      b. huge      c. active      d. amazing

**Completing
the Sentence**

*From the following list of words, choose the one that
best completes each of the sentences below. Write the
word in the space provided.*

## Group A

| | | | |
|---|---|---|---|
| dole | grit | vandalism | parody |
| titanic | burly | ambiguous | dumfounded |
| meteoric | maneuver | refurbish | rigorous |

1. Her reply was so _____ that I'm still not sure whether or not
   she is planning to attend our party.
2. The main reason Mother took that part-time job was to save money to
   _____ our household furnishings.
3. Between the halves of the football game, our marching band performed all
   kinds of _____ on the field as the crowd applauded.
4. At Holly's birthday party, Steve sang a clever _____ of an
   old song which he called "Hello, Holly!"
5. I had high hopes of making a lot of money at my summer job as a bellboy,
   but I found that most people _____ out tips very carefully.
6. Who would have expected a rather quiet and shy girl like Laura to show
   such _____ when the accident occurred!

## Group B

| | | | |
|---|---|---|---|
| compact | implement | pry | extinct |
| resourceful | scant | initiative | confer |
| formulate | stealthy | delude | rummage |

1. I spent an hour _____ around in the attic trying to find my
   old pair of ice skates.
2. Instead of waiting for someone to tell him what to do, Chet took the
   _____ and organized a rescue party on the spot.
3. At the exhibit of "Life in Colonial Days," we saw many quaint and old-
   fashioned _____ that people once used to perform
   everyday tasks.
4. "If we are to solve this problem once and for all," I observed, "we must
   first _____ an effective plan of attack."
5. The ten-cent hot dog that Father remembers from the "good old days" has
   become entirely _____ .

**6.** When I wasn't sure how to handle the job, I _____ with my boss about the proper procedures to follow.

**7.** To be successful in business, you must be _____ enough to find new ways of doing things when the old familiar ways no longer work.

---

### Word Families

**A.** *On the line provided, write a **noun form** for each of the following words.*

EXAMPLE: compact — **compactness**

**1.** delude _____

**2.** formulate _____

**3.** refurbish _____

**4.** rigorous _____

**5.** distort _____

**6.** extinct _____

**7.** inevitable _____

**8.** meteoric _____

**9.** prevail _____

**10.** replenish _____

**11.** abduct _____

**12.** ambiguous _____

**13.** confer _____

**14.** frigid _____

**15.** stealthy _____

**16.** strident _____

**17.** titanic _____

**18.** resourceful _____

**19.** burly _____

**20.** scant _____

**B.** *On the line provided, write a **verb** related to each of the following words.*

EXAMPLE: indisputable — **dispute**

**1.** fossil _____

**2.** vandalism _____

**3.** bumbling _____

**4.** initiative _____

**5.** abominable _____

**C.** On the line provided, give an **adjective** related to each of the following words.

EXAMPLE. maneuver — **maneuverable**

**1.** skimp _____

**2.** panorama _____

**3.** grit _____

**4.** prevail _____

**5.** consequence _____

---

**Filling the Blanks**  Encircle the pair of words that best complete the meaning of each of the following passages.

**1.** I am always _____ by the amazing powers of observation and deduction exhibited by my favorite _____ , the legendary Sherlock Holmes.
   a. deluded . . . fossil       c. dogged . . . vandal
   b. ingrained . . . foil       d. dumfounded . . . sleuth

**2.** "Although we have devised a plan to deal with the situation," the official said, "we will not be able to _____ it until we get the funds that the government has _____ for the project."
   a. replenish . . . conferred    c. refurbish . . . maneuvered
   b. implement . . . earmarked    d. formulate . . . rummaged

**3.** Though such animals as the saber-toothed tiger and the woolly mammoth have been _____ since the close of the last Ice Age, many thousands of years ago, their _____ remains have been found in various parts of the world.
   a. extinct . . . fossilized     c. skimpy . . . distorted
   b. scant . . . earmarked        d. indisputable . . . unerring

**4.** The way in which the nimble little star quarterback _____ around the _____ linebackers attempting to sack him reminded me of a bicycle weaving through heavy midtown traffic.
   a. engulfed . . . compact       c. maneuvered . . . burly
   b. abducted . . . strapping     d. foiled . . . frigid

**5.** A gang of terrorists had made plans to _____ the official and hold him for ransom. Fortunately, however, the police were able to _____ the plot after an informant tipped them off about it.
   a. delude . . . balk            c. sabotage . . . distort
   b. abduct . . . foil            d. parody . . . pry

# Cumulative Review Units 1–12

**Analogies** *In each of the following, encircle the item that best completes the comparison.*

**1. dumfounded** is to **shock** as
a. befuddled Is to confusion
b. irked is to pleasure
c. pacified is to disgust
d. infuriated is to satisfaction

**2. culprit** is to **commit** as
a. nonconformist is to obey
b. oaf is to foil
c. sage is to bungle
d. sleuth is to solve

**3. thrive** is to **wither** as
a. skimp is to restrict
b. idolize is to detest
c. reminisce is to recall
d. refute is to disprove

**4. vandalism** is to **destroy** as
a. initiative is to harm
b. fossil is to foil
c. sabotage is to wreck
d. memento Is to Injure

**5. serene** is to **ruffle** as
a. dogged is to persevere
b. gullible is to delude
c. resourceful is to motivate
d. valiant is to intimidate

**6. keepsake** is to **memento** as
a. agenda is to decision
b. fidelity is to treachery
c. fatality is to death
d. debut is to journey

**7. deluge** is to **engulf** as
a. blizzard is to bake
b. earthquake is to devastate
c. drought is to swamp
d. avalanche is to fry

**8. pitcher** is to **balk** as
a. sleuth is to commit
b. horse is to shy
c. vandal is to refurbish
d. elephant is to forget

**9. partisan** is to **defend** as
a. hypocrite is to pry
b. pacifist is to attack
c. vagabond is to tarry
d. oracle is to predict

**10. gory** is to **sight** as
a. sinister is to taste
b. meteoric is to feel
c. strident is to sound
d. martial is to smell

---

**Shades of Meaning** *Read each sentence carefully. Then encircle the item that best completes the statement below the sentence.*

Packing winds in excess of 100 miles per hour, hurricane Andrew tore through Florida in 1992, leaving wholesale devastation in its wake. **(2)**

**1.** In line 2 the word **devastation** most nearly means
a. grief      b. destruction      c. flooding      d. misery

After the Emancipation Proclamation of 1863, Union victories in the South were often occasions for the mass liberation of slaves. **(2)**

**2.** The word **liberation** in line 2 is used to mean
a. freeing      b. arrest      c. transportation   d. migration

In fencing matches the two competitors bring the tips of their foils together to signal that they are ready to commence. **(2)**

**3.** In line 1 the word **foils** is best defined as
a. weapons      b. pistols      c. daggers      d. swords

From a nearby hilltop scouts could see an enemy regiment drawn up in a long battle line at the forest's verge.

(2)

**4.** The word **verge** in line 2 most nearly means
- a. path
- b. clearing
- c. edge
- d. center

Riflemen preparing for battle thoroughly cleaned their weapons to make sure they were free of grit.

(2)

**5.** The best definition for the word **grit** in line 2 is
- a. courage
- b. determination
- c. mettle
- d. dirt

---

**Filling the Blanks**  *Encircle the pair of words that best complete the meaning of each of the following passages.*

1. That terrible _____ of war, like the atomic bomb, should in fact prove to be our most reliable guardians of the peace is one of the most puzzling _____ of modern life.
   - a. misgivings . . . consequences
   - b. vows . . . innovations
   - c. illusions . . . facets
   - d. implements . . . enigmas

2. Though a number of people claim to have spotted his tracks or even sighted him, the yeti, or "_____ snowman," has proved to be one of nature's most _____ creatures, and may not even exist!
   - a. burly . . . pathetic
   - b. abominable . . . elusive
   - c. immobile . . . incomprehensible
   - d. ingenious . . . ambiguous

3. "In the frozen wastes of Antarctica," the world-famous explorer remarked, "temperatures are so _____ that a person's hands and feet can become _____ with cold after only a brief exposure to the elements."
   - a. frigid . . . numb
   - b. acute . . . extinct
   - c. gross . . . sluggish
   - d. rigorous . . . null and void

4. Though the storm itself was of very brief _____ , it dumped so much snow on the city while it lasted that roads and highways all over town were virtually _____ for a week.
   - a. format . . . indisputable
   - b. onset . . . inflammatory
   - c. duration . . . impassable
   - d. stamina . . . incalculable

5. "I wouldn't go near that particular joint," I warned them, "because it is known to be a favorite _____ of hoods, pushers, and other _____ or disreputable characters."
   - a. terrain . . . smug
   - b. rendezvous . . . sinister
   - c. earmark . . . affluent
   - d. queue . . . petty

# Unit 13

**Definitions**

*Note carefully the spelling, pronunciation, and definition of each of the following words. Then write the word in the illustrative phrase following.*

**1. adhere**
(ad 'hēr)

(v.) to stick to, remain attached; to be devoted as a follower or supporter

_____ to our original plan

**2. affirm**
(ə 'fərm)

(v.) to declare to be true, state positively; to confirm

_____ my faith in human nature

**3. atrocity**
(ə 'träs ət ē)

(n.) an extremely wicked, brutal, or cruel act; something very bad or unpleasant

Nazi _____

**4. audition**
(ô 'dish ən)

(n.) a trial hearing for a performer;
(v.) to conduct or perform such a hearing

an _____ for the school play

**5. cope**
(kōp)

(v.) to struggle successfully against; to prove to be a match for, deal with satisfactorily; (n.) a long religious cloak; a canopy

_____ with a difficult situation

**6. deter**
(di 'tər)

(v.) to discourage or prevent through fear or doubt

laws to _____ jaywalkers

**7. disquieting**
(dis 'kwī ət iŋ)

(adj.) causing uneasiness or worry

a _____ development

**8. empower**
(em 'paú ər)

(v.) to give power or authority to; to enable; to permit

_____ her to sign the papers

**9. fluent**
('flü ənt)

(adj.) speaking or writing easily and smoothly, flowing gracefully

a _____ speaker

**10. lag**
(lag)

(v.) to move slowly or fall behind; (n.) a falling behind; the amount by which someone or something is behind; an interval

_____ behind the rest

**11. mangle**
('maŋ gəl)

(v.) to injure very seriously by cutting, tearing, crushing, etc.; to bring to ruin

_____ in the machinery

**12. misapprehension**
(mis ap ri 'hen shən)

(n.) a wrong idea, misunderstanding

the victim of a _____

**13. optimist**
('äp tə mist)

(n.) one who expects things to turn out for the best

the rosy view of an _____

**14. prowl**
(praŭl)

(v.) to roam about stealthily in search of something

_____ the jungle at night

**15. stupefy**
('stü pə fī)

(v.) to make stupid, dull, or groggy; to surprise or astonish

_____ by the extreme heat

**16. sulky**
('səl kē)

(adj.) in a bad or nasty mood, resentful; gloomy

a _____ child

**17. supplement**
('səp lə ment)

(n.) something added to complete a thing or make up for a lack; a section added to a book or document; (v.) to provide such an addition or completion

_____ our diet with vitamins

**18. surge**
(sərj)

(v.) to have a heavy, violent, swelling motion (like waves); (n.) a powerful forward rush

_____ ahead of the pack

**19. trait**
(trāt)

(n.) a quality or characteristic (especially of personality); a distinguishing feature

has many fine _____

**20. unscrupulous**
(ən 'skrü pyə ləs)

(adj.) dishonest; not guided or controlled by moral principles

will not deal with _____ merchants

---

**Completing the Sentence**

*Choose the word from this unit that best completes each of the following sentences. Write it in the space given.*

**1.** In spite of our best efforts, collections for the Community Fund this year have _____ far behind last year's figures.

**2.** When he gets in one of those _____ moods, he is as unreasonable and unpleasant as a cranky child.

**3.** If you are having so much trouble with a program of four major courses, how do you expect to _____ with a fifth course?

**4.** The unfavorable weather reports did not _____ us from holding the picnic that we had planned for so long.

**5.** Naturally we were upset when we received the _____ news that Uncle had been taken to the hospital.

**6.** The witness solemnly _____ that the evidence she was about to give was true.

**7.** Do you think that it is possible to become _____ in a foreign language without actually living in a country where it is spoken?

**8.** Now that the job has been completed, I have finally become skillful in

hanging the paper so that it _____ firmly to the wall.

**9.** It is hard to be a(n) _____ when everything goes against
you.

**10.** As soon as the doors were opened, the shoppers, eager for the advertised

bargains, _____ into the store in great waves.

**11.** As the robber _____ the streets looking for victims, he was
unaware that undercover police officers were watching his every move.

**12.** On Broadway, _____ that are open to any performer who
just walks in off the street are referred to as "cattle calls."

**13.** He is so careless in handling his textbooks that by the end of the term he

has practically _____ all of them.

**14.** Since she has a large family, she finds it necessary to _____
her income by working at a second job at night and on weekends.

**15.** We were so _____ by the bad news that for a few moments
we just sat there without moving or speaking.

**16.** In spite of all his talents, he will never gain high public office because so

many voters feel that he is _____ and cannot be trusted.

**17.** If you think that I would go to a party without being invited, you are under

a complete _____ .

**18.** The Constitution _____ the President to name the people
who will fill many of the most important positions in the government.

**19.** Throughout her long and noble career, her outstanding _____
has been her deep love for her fellow human beings.

**20.** Drunken soldiers roamed the streets of the fallen city, committing one

_____ after another on the terrified population.

---

**Synonyms**  *Choose the word from this unit that is most nearly **the
same** in meaning as each of the following groups of
expressions. Write the word on the line given.*

**1.** to damage, mutilate, butcher, disfigure  _____

**2.** grouchy, sullen, peevish, petulant  _____

**3.** an outrage, enormity, monstrosity  _____

**4.** a feature, quality, characteristic  _____

**5.** to trail, straggle, bring up the rear  _____

**6.** a misunderstanding, misconception  _____

**7.** to flood, rush, gush; a wave _____

**8.** someone who looks on the bright side of things _____

**9.** troubling, disturbing, alarming _____

**10.** a hearing, tryout, screen test _____

**11.** to make do, manage, get along, handle _____

**12.** to discourage, scare off, prevent _____

**13.** to stun, daze, shock, astonish, amaze _____

**14.** dishonest, crooked, corrupt, shady _____

**15.** an addition, extension; to add to _____

**16.** eloquent, articulate, glib; flowing _____

**17.** to rove, roam; to skulk, slink, lurk _____

**18.** to authorize, license, permit _____

**19.** to stick, cling, hold fast; to be loyal _____

**20.** to declare, assert; to confirm, ratify _____

---

**Antonyms**  *Choose the word from this unit that is most nearly **opposite** in meaning to each of the following groups of expressions. Write the word on the line given.*

**1.** to forbid, prohibit, ban, disqualify _____

**2.** a pessimist, Gloomy Gus, prophet of doom _____

**3.** cheerful, sociable, sunny, amiable _____

**4.** to unfasten, unglue; to abandon, betray _____

**5.** to awaken, arouse, stimulate, enliven _____

**6.** to keep up; to outstrip, outdo _____

**7.** fair, honest, trustworthy, aboveboard _____

**8.** to recede, ebb; a recession, slowdown _____

**9.** calming, reassuring, soothing, comforting _____

**10.** halting, tongue-tied; choppy _____

**11.** to encourage, urge on _____

**12.** to deny, disavow; to reject, veto, disallow _____

**13.** a good deed, kindness, kind act _____

**Choosing the Right Word**   *Encircle the **boldface** word that more satisfactorily completes each of the following sentences.*

1. When everything went wrong for Stan, and he saw absolutely no way out of his troubles, he muttered to himself, "I just can't (**mangle, cope**)!"

2. After the conductor (**auditioned, supplemented**) all the candidates for the position of first violinist, he made his final choice.

3. Jackals and other scavengers now (**prowl, deter**) through the ruins of what was once a great city.

4. I agree fully with what the previous speaker has said, but I should like to (**audition, supplement**) his ideas with a few remarks of my own.

5. There is no one (**surge, trait**) that makes him so likable; it is the overall effect of his personality.

6. Everything that I have learned about Abraham Lincoln from history books (**stupefies, affirms**) my reverence for this great President.

7. The City Council has approved funds for a new playground, but we expect a (**lag, surge**) of several months before construction begins.

8. The play went along smoothly until it came to Mark Antony's funeral oration, which Fred (**empowered, mangled**) beyond all recognition.

9. Come what may, I will (**adhere, surge**) to the great ideas and ideals for which our ancestors suffered so much.

10. Although José has been living in this country for only a few years, I would love to be half as (**fluent, sulky**) in Spanish as he is in English.

11. A loud groan went through the class when we got the (**unscrupulous, disquieting**) news that there would be a full-period test later in the week.

12. The worst way to deal with disappointments is to become (**fluent, sulky**); the best way is to smile and make up your mind to try again.

13. All those smooth words and vague promises are not going to (**empower, deter**) us from doing what we know is needed to improve conditions.

14. Jim took one look at the statue I fashioned from stray pieces of junk and exclaimed, "That's not a sculpture; it's a(n) (**lag, atrocity**)!"

15. My definition of a(n) (**optimist, misapprehension**) is someone who looks at an almost empty bottle of juice and says, "This bottle is one-quarter *full*."

16. Who (**deterred, empowered**) you to speak for everyone in our class?

17. A true friend would not have been so (**sulky, unscrupulous**) as to take unfair advantage of your trust and confidence.

18. It is far better to know you are ignorant of something than to act on the basis of wrong information and (**misapprehensions, auditions**).

19. Shortly after World War II, Japan began the great economic (**surge, lag**) that has put her among the world's top industrial nations.

20. Have all these years of peace and good living (**disquieted, stupefied**) us to such an extent that we are not even prepared to defend ourselves?

# Unit 14

**Definitions**

*Note carefully the spelling, pronunciation, and definition of each of the following words. Then write the word in the blank space in the illustrative phrase following.*

**1. abstain**
(ab 'stān)

(v.) to stay away from doing something by one's own choice

_____ from fattening foods

**2. accommodate**
(ə 'käm ə dāt)

(v.) to do a favor or service for, help out; to provide for, supply with; to have space for; to make fit or suitable

room to _____ six people

**3. allegiance**
(ə 'lēj əns)

(n.) the loyalty or obligation owed to a government, nation, cause, etc.

swore _____ to their country

**4. amalgamate**
(ə 'mal gə māt)

(v.) to unite; to combine elements into a unified whole

_____ two small companies into a large corporation

**5. append**
(ə 'pend)

(v.) to attach or add as a supplement or extra item

_____ a list of readings to the text

**6. commemorate**
(kə 'mem ə rāt)

(v.) to preserve, honor, or celebrate the memory of

_____ Washington's birthday

**7. enumerate**
(i 'nü mə rāt)

(v.) to count; to name one by one, list

_____ the benefits of the plan

**8. exalt**
(eg 'zôlt)

(v.) to make high in rank, power, character, or quality; to fill with pride, joy, or noble feeling; to praise, honor

whom Fortune has _____ to such high position

**9. extort**
(ek 'stôrt)

(v.) to obtain by violence, misuse of authority, or threats

_____ ransom money

**10. far-fetched**
('fär 'fecht)

(adj.) strained or improbable (in the sense of not being logical or believable), going far afield from a topic

a _____ excuse

**11. glum**
(gləm)

(adj.) depressed, gloomy

a _____ expression on one's face

**12. replica**
('rep lə kə)

(n.) a copy, close reproduction

made a _____ of the Mayflower

**13. responsive**
(ri 'spän siv)

(adj.) answering or replying; reacting readily to requests, suggestions, etc.; showing interest and understanding

_____ to their wishes

**14. sanctuary**
('saŋk chə wer ē)

(*n.*) a sacred or holy place; refuge or protection from capture or punishment; a place of refuge or protection

built the altar in the _____

**15. self-seeking**
(self 'sēk iŋ)

(*adj.*) selfishly ambitious

a _____ politician

**16. submissive**
(səb 'mis iv)

(*adj.*) humbly obedient; tending to give in to authority, obeying without protest

a totally _____ attitude

**17. tally**
('tal ē)

(*v.*) to count up; to keep score; to make entries for reckoning; to correspond or agree; (*n.*) a total or score

_____ the results of the tournament

**18. taskmaster**
('task mas tər)

(*n.*) one whose job it is to assign work to others; one who uses his or her power to make people work very hard

a harsh _____

**19. transform**
(trans 'fôrm)

(*v.*) to change completely in appearance or form; to make into something else

totally _____ the countryside

**20. upheaval**
(əp 'hēv əl)

(*n.*) a sudden, violent upward movement; great disorder or radical change

a social and economic _____

---

**Completing the Sentence**
*Choose the word from this unit that best completes each of the following sentences. Write it in the space given.*

**1.** In just a few years, she had been _____ from an awkward tomboy into a charming young woman.

**2.** Anne usually seems to be quiet and _____ , but she has a way of flaring up when she feels that anyone is being unfair to her.

**3.** I enjoyed the first part of the detective story, but the surprise ending was so _____ that I couldn't accept it.

**4.** I would like to _____ you, but I don't think it is right to allow you to copy my homework.

**5.** A portion of the forest has been set aside as a bird _____ for the protection of endangered species in the area.

**6.** When Ben Franklin said, "God helps those who help themselves," he did *not* mean that the most important thing in life is to be _____ .

**7.** When we visited New York City, we bought a small _____ of the Statue of Liberty as a memento of our trip.

**8.** I love basketball games, but I have decided to _____ from attending them until I can get my grades up to where they should be.

**9.** Remember that the Oath of _____ is not a formula to be repeated mechanically but a summary of our sacred duty to our country.

**10.** Can you see why it was logical for various labor unions in the clothing and textile industries to _____ into a single organization?

**11.** Under our Constitution, officials are never _____ to a point where they are more important or more powerful than the law.

**12.** Is there anything more despicable than trying to _____ money from innocent people by threatening them with bodily harm?

**13.** Imagine how _____ we felt when a sudden wave of warm weather melted all the snow and ruined our plans for a winter carnival!

**14.** Though an injured hand kept Larry from actually bowling, he took part in the tournament by keeping a careful _____ of the scores.

**15.** Good employees don't need a(n) _____ to keep them working.

**16.** Every entertainer likes a(n) _____ audience that shows it appreciates and enjoys a performance.

**17.** I know that Mother has given you all kinds of instructions before you leave for camp, but let me _____ some extra advice of my own.

**18.** We learned in our science class how _____ of the earth's crust have resulted in the formation of mountains.

**19.** The driving instructor _____ carefully the bad habits and practices that are likely to lead to accidents.

**20.** On Memorial Day, Americans gather in ceremonies across the country to _____ the nation's war dead.

---

**Synonyms**  Choose the word from this unit that is most nearly **the same** in meaning as each of the following groups of expressions. Write the word on the line given.

**1.** to elevate, raise; to uplift  _____

**2.** to list, check off, spell out, specify  _____

**3.** unlikely, improbable, hard to swallow  _____

**4.** a copy, duplicate, reproduction, imitation  _____

**5.** selfish, opportunistic, gold-digging  _____

**6.** a holy place, shrine; a haven; refuge  _____

**7.** a supervisor, overseer; a slave driver  _____

**8.** loyalty, obedience, devotion, fidelity  _____

**9.** to avoid, decline, resist, refrain from  _____

**10.** to combine, merge, consolidate  _____

**11.** to add, attach, tack on  _____

**12.** to honor, memorialize, celebrate  _____

**13.** meek, compliant, servile, subservient  _____

**14.** to oblige, help; to lodge, house; to adapt  _____

**15.** confusion, disruption, chaos  _____

**16.** to blackmail, coerce, bilk, "shake down"  _____

**17.** gloomy, dejected, morose, melancholy  _____

**18.** to change, alter, convert  _____

**19.** a score; to total; to record; to agree  _____

**20.** sympathetic to, open to, receptive to  _____

---

**Antonyms**  *Choose the word from this unit that is most nearly **opposite** in meaning to each of the following groups of expressions. Write the word on the line given.*

**1.** to divide, separate, carve up, break up  _____

**2.** to cast down, humble, degrade, demote, depose  _____

**3.** rebellious, defiant, insubordinate  _____

**4.** peace and quiet, tranquillity  _____

**5.** insensitive, unsympathetic, slow to respond  _____

**6.** likely, probable, plausible, credible  _____

**7.** an original, prototype  _____

**8.** unselfish, selfless, altruistic  _____

**9.** to maintain, preserve unchanged  _____

**10.** to yield to, give in to; indulge in  _____

**11.** to detach from, disconnect  _____

**12.** to dishonor; to forget, overlook  _____

**13.** to disoblige, inconvenience, trouble  _____

**14.** cheerful, merry, rosy, sunny  _____

**Choosing the Right Word**  *Encircle the **boldface** word that more satisfactorily completes each of the following sentences.*

1. It remains to be seen how (**responsive, glum**) the students will be to the new method of teaching mathematics.

2. The new hotel is spacious enough to (**accommodate, extort**) large groups of people attending conventions and banquets.

3. Experience has taught me that people who constantly boast about their unselfishness are often secretly quite (**submissive, self-seeking**).

4. Only seven members of the Security Council voted on the resolution; the others (**abstained, appended**).

5. The detective's suspicion was aroused when the suspect's story failed to (**tally, append**) with the known facts of the case.

6. Financiers are planning to (**extort, amalgamate**) various businesses in the United States and England into one huge multinational corporation.

7. When he felt low, he found that reading the Bible (**exalted, appended**) his spirits.

8. Each member of the basketball team was awarded a trophy to (**transform, commemorate**) the championship season.

9. The Mayor had to choose between (**allegiance, tally**) to his political party and his judgment of what was best for the city.

10. The United States has a long history of providing (**upheaval, sanctuary**) to those fleeing the persecution of tyrannical regimes abroad.

11. Isn't it a little (**far-fetched, self-seeking**) to suggest that the pollution of our environment is mainly caused by creatures from outer space?

12. Since she sets extremely high standards for herself and is always pushing herself to do better, she is her own most severe (**taskmaster, replica**).

13. Unless the poor people of that country see some hope of improving their lives, there will probably soon be a great social (**allegiance, upheaval**) there.

14. I didn't have time to write a letter to Lucy, but I (**appended, enumerated**) a few sentences to my sister's letter, expressing my congratulations.

15. He enjoys (**abstaining, enumerating**) all the factors that enabled him to rise from poverty to great wealth, but he always omits one—good luck.

16. Shelley Wilentz is the kind of manager who does not try to (**extort, exalt**) cooperation from the people under her, but *earns* it by being a real leader.

17. If you look so (**far-fetched, glum**) just because you can't go to the party, how are you going to react when something really bad happens?

18. Instead of working so hard to prepare (**replicas, allegiances**) of famous works of art, why don't you try to create something original of your own?

19. In Robert Louis Stevenson's classic story, a chemical potion (**tallies, transforms**) the good Dr. Jekyll into the evil Mr. Hyde.

20. We cannot have a peaceful and just society so long as any one race is required to be (**responsive, submissive**) to another.

**Definitions** *Note carefully the spelling, pronunciation, and definition of each of the following words. Then write the word in the blank space in the illustrative phrase following.*

**1. beacon**
('bē kən)

(n.) a light or other signal that warns and guides; a lighthouse; anything that guides or inspires

a _____ in the dark night

**2. berserk**
(bər 'sərk)

(adj., adv.) violently and destructively enraged

a _____ gunman

**3. celestial**
(sə 'les chəl)

(adj.) having to do with the sky or heavens; heavenly; yielding great bliss or happiness

a _____ being

**4. chasten**
('chā sən)

(v.) to punish (in order to bring about improvement in behavior, attitude, etc.); to restrain, moderate

_____ the balky child

**5. confiscate**
('kän fə skāt)

(v.) to seize by authority; to take and keep

_____ the car used in the holdup

**6. data**
('dā to)

(pl. n.) information; facts

studied all the available _____

**7. detract**
(di 'trakt)

(v.) to take away from; reduce in value or reputation

_____ from your natural beauty

**8. encounter**
(en 'kaün tər)

(n.) a meeting (especially one that is unplanned); a meeting of enemies, battle; (v.) to meet or come upon

_____ many dangers

**9. epic**
('ep ik)

(n.) a long narrative poem (or other literary composition) about the deeds of heroes; an event or movement of great sweep; (adj.) on a grand scale, vast

an _____ struggle

**10. pantomime**
('pan tə mīm)

(n.) a play or story performed without words by actors using only gestures; (v.) to express in this way

since ballet relies heavily on _____

**11. pessimist**
('pes ə mist)

(n.) one who believes or expects the worst

neither an optimist nor a _____

**12. precaution**
(pri 'kô shən)

(n.) care taken beforehand; a step or action taken to prevent something from happening

sensible _____ against fire

**13. prosecute**
('präs ə kyüt)

(v.) to bring before a court of law for trial; to carry out

_____ the accused

**14. puncture**
('pəŋk chər)

(*n.*) a small hole made by a sharp object; (*v.*) to make such a hole, pierce

_____ the bag with an ice pick

**15. retaliate**
(ri 'tal ē āt)

(*v.*) to get revenge; to strike back for an injury

_____ for the insult

**16. sham**
(sham)

(*adj.*) fake, not genuine; (*n.*) something false pretending to be genuine; a pretender; a decorated pillow covering; (*v.*) to pretend

a _____ attack

**17. uncouth**
(ən 'küth)

(*adj.*) unrefined, crude; awkward or clumsy

an _____ appearance

**18. underscore**
('ən dər skôr)

(*v.*) to draw a line under; to put special emphasis on; (*n.*) a line drawn under something

_____ the need for prompt action

**19. wholesome**
('hōl səm)

(*adj.*) healthy; morally and socially sound and good; helping to bring about or preserve good health

_____ food

**20. wistful**
('wist fəl)

(*adj.*) full of melancholy yearning or longing, sad

a _____ look

---

**Completing the Sentence**

*Choose the word from this unit that best completes each of the following sentences. Write it in the space given.*

**1.** In polite society it is considered _____ to balance peas on your knife at the dinner table.

**2.** Late that afternoon, one of the inmates went _____ and totally wrecked the infirmary.

**3.** When she said she would "turn the other cheek," she simply meant that she would not _____ for the injury done to her.

**4.** In ancient times, people gazed at the sky and studied the planets and other _____ bodies to predict the future.

**5.** In the old days, whippings and other forms of physical punishment were used to _____ student misbehavior, even in college.

**6.** Although he could speak no English, he made us understand by the use of _____ that he was extremely thirsty.

**7.** Over the years, a great many ships have been saved from destruction by that tall _____ standing on the rocky coast.

**8.** Isn't it remarkable that a(n) _____ poem such as the *Iliad*, written almost 3,000 years ago, still has interest for readers today?

**9.** Nothing can _____ from the fact that he stood by us in our hour of greatest need.

**10.** Before we use the blowtorch in our industrial arts class, we are required to take the _____ of wearing goggles.

**11.** So there I was with a(n) _____ in one of my rear tires, on a lonely road, on a dark night, and during a violent rainstorm!

**12.** My definition of a(n) _____ is someone who worries about the hole in the doughnut and forgets about the cake surrounding it.

**13.** After the war, all the property that had been _____ by the government was turned back to its former owners.

**14.** Now that we have gathered a vast amount of _____ , it is up to us to draw some useful conclusions from all this information.

**15.** With a(n) _____ expression on his face, the prisoner looked through his cell window at the patch of sky that meant freedom to him.

**16.** Freedom of speech is a(n) _____ and a mockery if it does not apply to people whose opinions are very unpopular.

**17.** The directions in the workbook instruct the user to _____ the subject of each sentence in red and the predicate in blue.

**18.** Little did I realize when I _____ that old man on a lonely beach that this chance meeting would change my life.

**19.** Though many people doubted that the new program would do any real good, I thought it was a very _____ development.

**20.** The police have done their job in arresting the suspect; now it is up to the district attorney to _____ him and prove his guilt.

---

**Synonyms**      *Choose the word from this unit that is most nearly **the same** in meaning as each of the following groups of expressions. Write the word on the line given.*

**1.** to subtract from, lower, reduce       _____

**2.** mad, enraged, deranged       _____

**3.** to meet, happen upon; a confrontation       _____

**4.** to underline, stress, emphasize, accent       _____

**5.** to put on trial; to pursue, carry on       _____

**6.** longing, yearning, melancholy, pensive       _____

**7.** a dumb show, charade, mime show       _____

**8.** facts, figures, statistics; information

**9.** phony, counterfeit; a fake; to pretend

**10.** a hole, perforation; to pierce

**11.** to avenge, get even with, pay back

**12.** healthy, nourishing; sound; beneficial

**13.** a prophet of doom, killjoy

**14.** heavenly, ethereal, stellar; blissful

**15.** a lighthouse, beam, signal, flare

**16.** to discipline, punish; to temper, restrain

**17.** a saga, chronicle; vast, titanic

**18.** foresight, prudence; a safeguard

**19.** to seize, commandeer, expropriate

**20.** crude, boorish; graceless, awkward

---

**Antonyms**    *Choose the word from this unit that is most nearly* **opposite** *in meaning to each of the following groups of expressions. Write the word on the line given.*

**1.** an optimist, Pollyanna

**2.** to increase, heighten, enhance

**3.** earthly, terrestrial; infernal

**4.** the genuine article; bona fide, authentic

**5.** harmful, unhealthy, baneful

**6.** sane, rational

**7.** to return, restore

**8.** to downplay, de-emphasize, soft-pedal

**9.** cheerful, happy, contented, satisfied

**10.** to avoid, sidestep

**11.** to praise, commend, reward

**12.** refined, polished, graceful, genteel

**13.** to pardon, forgive, turn the other cheek

**14.** recklessness, heedlessness

**15.** to defend; to abandon, give up

**Choosing the Right Word**  *Encircle in the parentheses the word that more satisfactorily completes each of the following sentences.*

1. She had such a (**celestial, sham**) expression on her face that I thought she'd had a vision of heaven.

2. The settlement of the American West is one of the great (**pantomimes, epics**) of world history.

3. I knew that it would be difficult to raise funds for the recycling program, but I never expected to (**chasten, encounter**) so many tough problems.

4. Her writing style is a little (**celestial, uncouth**), but what it lacks in polish and refinement is more than made up for by its wonderful humor.

5. During the long years of defeat, Lincoln searched for a general who would (**prosecute, retaliate**) the war fearlessly until the Union was saved.

6. Marie is not really pretty, but her sparkling personality and (**wholesome, berserk**) charm make her very attractive.

7. If you try to smuggle goods into this country without paying the customs duties, the inspectors may (**puncture, confiscate**) the goods and fine you.

8. The youth center that the charity organized was like a(n) (**epic, beacon**) to many young people desperately needing help and guidance.

9. The report that he sent to the president of the company (**underscored, retaliated**) the need for better planning and more careful use of funds.

10. The news that I had been dropped from the football squad (**detracted, punctured**) my dream of becoming a great gridiron hero.

11. Is it right to (**retaliate, confiscate**) against an evil act by performing evil acts of one's own?

12. For some strange reason, the photocopier suddenly went (**berserk, sham**) and started spewing vast quantities of paper all over the floor.

13. As I watched through the soundproof hospital window, the skaters on the pond seemed to be carrying out a colorful (**pantomime, epic**).

14. The child gazed (**wistfully, wholesomely**) at the shiny toys in the store window.

15. The Bible tells us that the Lord is like a stern but loving parent, and that "whom He loveth, He (**chasteneth, detracteth**)."

16. Many a perfectly healthy employee has been known to (**retaliate, sham**) illness to avoid going to work.

17. Before we can plan properly for the upcoming school year, we must have accurate (**beacons, data**) on the results of last year's programs.

18. It does not (**prosecute, detract**) in the least from his reputation as a great player to say that all the team members deserve equal credit.

19. Our driving instructor has emphasized that the use of seat belts is not just a "silly" (**encounter, precaution**) but a surefire way of saving lives.

20. The trouble with being a(n) (**epic, pessimist**) is that you are so taken up with what is going wrong that you are unaware of what is going right.

# Review Units 13–15

**Analogies**　　In each of the following, encircle the item that best completes the comparison.

**1. optimist** is to **pessimist** as
a. trait is to characteristic
b. original is to replica
c. outrage is to atrocity
d. sham is to fake

**2. beacon** is to **light** as
a. shoe is to foot
b. mailbox is to letter
c. hydrant is to water
d. step is to ladder

**3. epic** is to **deeds** as
a. lyric is to emotions
b. novel is to desires
c. play is to goals
d. opera is to ambitions

**4. pantomime** is to **speak** as
a. symphony is to play
b. ballet is to sing
c. drama is to act
d. comedy is to laugh

**5. crook** is to **unscrupulous** as
a. swindler is to berserk
b. optimist is to glum
c. diplomat is to uncouth
d. manipulator is to self-seeking

**6. celestial** is to **heaven** as
a. marine is to sky
b. colonial is to sea
c. terrestrial is to earth
d. urban is to country

**7. wholesome** is to **favorable** as
a. far-fetched is to unfavorable
b. self-seeking is to favorable
c. responsive is to unfavorable
d. glum is to favorable

**8. boor** is to **uncouth** as
a. celebrity is to unknown
b. genius is to unthinking
c. star is to unpopular
d. savage is to uncivilized

**9. pin** is to **puncture** as
a. saw is to chop
b. knife is to cut
c. rope is to release
d. ax is to drench

**10. monument** is to **commemorate** as
a. trash basket is to guide
b. lamppost is to deter
c. crosswalk is to transform
d. milestone is to mark

**11. data** are to **inform** as
a. jokes are to amuse
b. headlines are to confuse
c. directions are to entertain
d. ideas are to puzzle

**12. amazement** is to **stupefy** as
a. praise is to chasten
b. confusion is to bewilder
c. boredom is to enthuse
d. puzzlement is to exalt

**13. allegiance** is to **adhere** as
a. time is to avoid
b. support is to dislike
c. blessing is to approve
d. consent is to refuse

**14. defeat** is to **glum** as
a. setback is to joyful
b. victory is to jubilant
c. failure is to happy
d. success is to sulky

**15. audition** is to **hear** as
a. preview is to see
b. misapprehension is to know
c. sanctuary is to feel
d. pantomime is to touch

**16. disquieting** is to **disturb** as
a. boring is to delight
b. amazing is to depress
c. astounding is to stupefy
d. heartrending is to amuse

**17. underscore** is to **line** as
a. tally is to arrow
b. encircle is to ring
c. box is to triangle
d. check is to dot

**18. cat** is to **prowl** as
a. horse is to neigh
b. goat is to butt
c. ostrich is to fly
d. snake is to slither

**R**

**19. supplement** is to **more** as
a. append is to less
b. cope is to more
c. detract is to less
d. lag is to more

**20. lineup** is to **enumerate** as
a. scorecard is to tally
b. ticket is to commemorate
c. program is to mangle
d. banner is to retaliate

---

**Identification**  *In each of the following groups, encircle the word that is best defined or suggested by the introductory expression.*

**1.** "Before we make a decision, we must have the facts, all the facts, and nothing but the facts."
a. tally          b. data          c. atrocity          d. misapprehension

**2.** joined the competing companies to form one huge business organization
a. amalgamate     b. affirm        c. exalt             d. accommodate

**3.** At 2:30, violinists seeking a position with the Symphony Orchestra will have a chance to play for the Director.
a. audition       b. pantomime     c. supplement        d. mangle

**4.** The knights swore lifelong loyalty to King Richard the Lion-hearted.
a. beacon         b. allegiance    c. tally             d. trait

**5.** "That costly failure taught me that I'm not as smart as I thought I was."
a. chasten        b. accommodate   c. surge             d. fluent

**6.** acted out in silence
a. atrocity       b. encounter     c. pantomime         d. precaution

**7.** great disorder and dislocation caused by a revolution
a. sham           b. upheaval      c. sanctuary         d. beacon

**8.** walked the streets of the city searching for helpless victims
a. surge          b. deter         c. prowl             d. retaliate

**9.** "Things are bad, and all the signs are that they're going to get worse."
a. pessimist      b. taskmaster    c. celestial         d. optimist

**10.** "Unless you pay me $500, I'm going to make trouble for you."
a. adhere         b. extort        c. enumerate         d. underscore

**11.** She speaks French like a native.
a. upheaval       b. supplement    c. fluent            d. data

**12.** "What an amazing piece of work—an exact reproduction, only 3 feet long, of an aircraft carrier!"
a. replica        b. trait         c. sanctuary         d. epic

**13.** a measure taken in advance to prevent an accident
a. precaution     b. allegiance    c. puncture          d. encounter

**14.** That man does not seem to have any morals when it comes to business.
a. submissive     b. glum          c. unscrupulous      d. wistful

**15.** what a district attorney does with a legal case
a. commemorate    b. prosecute     c. confiscate        d. enumerate

**16.** He is only interested in people for what he can get out of them.
a. sulky          b. berserk       c. disquieting       d. self-seeking

**Shades of Meaning**   *Read each sentence carefully. Then encircle the item that best completes the statement below the sentence.*

An encounter in 1959 between Vice President Richard Nixon and Soviet Premier Nikita Khruschev over the merits of the market economy has come to be known as the "kitchen debate."

**1.** In line 1 the word **encounter** most nearly means
a. confrontation
b. agreement
c. chance meeting
d. brawl

Flashing a sham police shield, the brazen intruder waltzed through the security checkpoint.

**2.** The word **sham** in line 1 is used to mean
a. genuine
b. plastic
c. fake
d. expired

When men first walked on the moon on July 20, 1969, newspapers across the country published supplements devoted to the historic event.

**3.** In line 2 the word **supplements** is best defined as
a. extra sections
b. photographs
c. editorials
d. articles

When civil war broke out in 1861, tens of thousands were responsive to calls for volunteers that issued from Washington and Richmond.

**4.** The phrase **were responsive to** in line 1 most nearly means
a. received
b. understood
c. appreciated
d. answered

Who would have guessed that the discovery of a minor break-in at the Watergate complex would lead to a scandal of such epic proportions?

**5.** In line 2 the word **epic** is best defined as
a. poetic
b. vast
c. fantastic
d. tragic

---

**Antonyms**   *In each of the following groups, encircle the word or expression that is most nearly **opposite** in meaning to the word in **boldface type** in the introductory phrase.*

**1.** designed to **deter** such practices
a. finance   b. encourage   c. study   d. stop

**2.** found the old neighborhood totally **transformed**
a. ruined   b. empty   c. unchanged   d. improved

**3.** **uncouth** behavior
a. criminal   b. strange   c. silly   d. genteel

**4.** **disquieting** news
a. disturbing   b. unexpected   c. comforting   d. latest

**5.** a **glum** expression on her face
a. cheerful     b. strange     c. sad     d. typical

**6.** **detract from** your appearance
a. change     b. enhance     c. study     d. hurt

**7.** **affirm** our rights in the case
a. examine     b. describe     c. defend     d. deny

**8.** a **far-fetched** excuse
a. lame     b. plausible     c. wordy     d. foolish

**9.** a **celestial** being
a. heavenly     b. beautiful     c. infernal     d. invisible

**10.** **unscrupulous** merchants
a. honest     b. wealthy     c. clever     d. troublesome

**11.** an **exalted** position in life
a. pleasant     b. new     c. lowly     d. high

**12.** a **wholesome** development
a. harmful     b. recent     c. surprising     d. desirable

**13.** wartime **atrocities**
a. crimes     b. supplies     c. fatalities     d. kindnesses

**14.** a **submissive** student
a. foreign     b. defiant     c. trustworthy     d. intelligent

**15.** **prosecute** the accused
a. defend     b. arrest     c. try     d. jail

---

**Completing the Sentence**

*From the following lists of words, choose the one that best completes each of the sentences below. Write the word in the space provided.*

**Group A**

| | | | |
|---|---|---|---|
| cope | stupefy | taskmaster | data |
| tally | extort | optimist | retaliate |

**1.** I was so _____ by the unexpected bad news that I could hardly speak.

**2.** I had to give up counting sheep as a means of falling asleep because I became too tired to _____ them accurately.

**3.** He expects us to work long hours every day and to keep going every minute without a letup. What a(n) _____ !

**4.** As secretary of the club, it is my job to keep accurate _____ on attendance at meetings, payment of dues, and other matters.

**5.** Even though he was unfair to you, you should not try to _____ by being equally unfair to him.

### Group B

| transform | pantomime | wistful | accommodate |
|-----------|-----------|---------|-------------|
| trait | surge | prosecute | underscore |

1. We will continue to _____ our campaign against air pollution until we have accomplished what we set out to do.
2. It is the duty of everyone—and I _____ the word *everyone* —to join in helping to make the Community Fund drive a success.
3. What a(n) _____ expression on poor Sue's face when she learned she would not be able to accompany us on the European trip!
4. The one _____ that, more than any other, accounts for her success is her ability to get along with other people.
5. When we asked Tom how he expected to travel, he didn't say a word but did a(n) _____ of getting on and riding his new bicycle.

### Word Families

A. *On the line provided, write a* **noun form** *of each of the following words.*

EXAMPLE: glum — **glumness**

1. adhere _____
2. affirm _____
3. deter _____
4. fluent _____
5. prowl _____
6. stupefy _____
7. sulky _____
8. unscrupulous _____
9. abstain _____
10. accommodate _____
11. append _____

B. *On the line provided, write an* **adjective** *related to each of the following.*

EXAMPLE: adhere — **adhesive**

1. atrocity _____
2. affirm _____
3. supplement _____
4. commemorate _____
5. pessimist _____

**C.** *On the line provided, write a **verb** related to each of the following words.*

EXAMPLE: audition — **audit**

1. misapprehension _____
2. sulky _____
3. responsive _____
4. submissive _____
5. replica _____

---

**Filling the Blanks**

*Encircle the pair of words that best complete the meaning of each of the following passages.*

1. There's a wise old saying that a(n) _____ sees a partially filled glass of water as half full, while a(n) _____ sees the same glass of water as half empty.
   a. taskmaster . . . sham
   b. optimist . . . pessimist
   c. replica . . . tally
   d. trait . . . beacon

2. The *Iliad*, Homer's famous _____ poem about the Trojan War, opens with the hero, Achilles, _____ moodily in his tent because he has not been accorded the proper reward for his brave deeds.
   a. pantomime . . . prowling
   b. atrocity . . . shamming
   c. epic . . . sulking
   d. beacon . . . lagging

3. "The only way we are going to _____ people from driving a car while drunk," the speaker observed, "is to impose stiff penalties on such behavior and _____ offenders to the full extent of the law."
   a. empower . . . accommodate
   b. detract . . . chasten
   c. exalt . . . puncture
   d. deter . . . prosecute

4. The _____ who had been lurking very suspiciously around the neighborhood was caught in the act of breaking into our house. The police _____ the set of burglar's tools that he had with him as evidence to back up the charges against him.
   a. prowler . . . confiscated
   b. optimist . . . underscored
   c. sham . . . mangled
   d. pessimist . . . enumerated

5. When we pledge _____ to our flag, we _____ our loyalty and devotion to the country and form of government for which it stands.
   a. precaution . . . commemorate
   b. data . . . underscore
   c. allegiance . . . affirm
   d. misapprehension . . . supplement

# Cumulative Review  Units 1–15

**Analogies**  *In each of the following, encircle the item that best completes the comparison.*

1. **allegiance** is to **devoted** as
a. support is to disinterested
b. ingenuity is to arid
c. fidelity is to faithful
d. favor is to submissive

2. **prowl** is to **stealthy** as
a. amble is to hasty
b. saunter is to leisurely
c. maneuver is to inept
d. lag is to strident

3. **wistful** is to **sadness** as
a. glum is to gloom
b. sheepish is to confidence
c. sluggish is to speed
d. frigid is to warmth

4. **stupefy** is to **dumfounded** as
a. infuriate is to jubilant
b. motivate is to chastened
c. delude is to resourceful
d. irk is to irritated

5. **adapter** is to **transform** as
a. mangle is to puncture
b. compactor is to compress
c. foil is to conserve
d. manacle is to topple

6. **rigorous** is to **stamina** as
a. adverse is to sincerity
b. inevitable is to discretion
c. gross is to initiative
d. intensive is to concentration

7. **sulky** is to **resentment** as
a. contrite is to remorse
b. responsive is to boredom
c. jovial is to anger
d. headstrong is to obedience

8. **surge** is to **forward** as
a. billow is to back
b. deter is to forward
c. recede is to back
d. constrain is to forward

9. **berserk** is to **control** as
a. logical is to clarity
b. numb is to sensation
c. nimble is to skill
d. dogged is to persistence

10. **adhere** is to **forsake** as
a. amalgamate is to partition
b. avenge is to retaliate
c. prevaricate is to dissect
d. waylay is to liberate

---

**Shades of Meaning**  *Read each sentence carefully. Then encircle the item that best completes the statement below the sentence.*

Can you name the artist who prophesied that in the future everyone would experience a dole of fame—15 minutes' worth, to be exact?  **(2)**

1. The word **dole** in line 2 is used to mean
a. small portion
b. handout
c. allowance
d. staggering amount

The opening scene of the play is set in a run-down waterfront saloon frequented by hoodlums and petty thieves.  **(2)**

2. In line 2 the word **petty** most nearly means
a. narrow-minded
b. piddling
c. big-time
d. small-time

Scattered over the Gettysburg battlefield are monuments exalting the men —both Southerner and Yankee—who fought and died there.  **(2)**

3. The word **exalting** in line 1 most nearly means
a. elevating    b. honoring    c. uplifting    d. naming

I didn't realize that the history text I had purchased was a used one until I opened it and found underscores on every other page. (2)

**4.** In line 2 the word **underscores** is defined as
    a. overrulings    b. mistakes    c. notes    d. underlinings

"Then breeze with sea commenced to flirt
And ruffles trimmed the water's skirt." ( A.E. Glug, "Flotsam and Jetsam") (2)

**5.** The best definition for the word **ruffles** in line 1 is
    a. driftwood    b. sand castles    c. ripples    d. seaweed

---

**Filling the Blanks**      *Encircle the pair of words that best complete each of the following passages.*

**1.** There were so many _____ on both sides during the battle of Antietam that it was the _____ conflict of the Civil War.
    a. enigmas . . . smuggest
    b. setbacks . . . pettiest
    c. fatalities . . . goriest
    d. assailants . . . eeriest

**2.** The district attorney decided not to _____ the case when it became clear that the evidence against the accused was too slight to win anything but his _____ .
    a. prosecute . . . acquittal
    b. formulate . . . reimbursement
    c. supplement . . . compliance
    d. implement . . . ingratitude

**3.** In classical times, the great temple of Apollo at Delphi housed the most famous _____ in all Greece. Deep within the confines of this ancient _____ , a priestess sitting on a golden tripod revealed the will of the gods to all who sought her assistance.
    a. sage . . . queue
    b. panorama . . . terrain
    c. beacon . . . fossil
    d. oracle . . . sanctuary

**4.** Some modern scientists believe that the _____ with which a gigantic meteor crashed into the Earth millions of years ago set off the chain of events that led to the _____ of the dinosaurs and the close of the Age of Reptiles.
    a. misgiving . . . diversity
    b. impact . . . extinction
    c. leeway . . . duration
    d. precaution . . . affluence

**5.** According to Greek myth, Theseus was able to find his way back out of the Labyrinth, a(n) _____ of passages and galleries built to house a fearful monster, by following a(n) _____ of wool that he had slowly unrolled from a large ball as he penetrated deeper and deeper into the bowels of the confusing building.
    a. rendezvous . . . barrage
    b. format . . . earmark
    c. maze . . . strand
    d. agenda . . . facet

# Final Mastery Test

**I. Selecting Word Meanings** *In each of the following groups, select the word or expression that is most nearly **the same** in meaning as the word in **boldface type** in the introductory phrase.*

**1.** had many **misgivings**
a. setbacks    b. doubts    c. victories    d. presents

**2. denounce** as a traitor
a. seize    b. betray    c. sentence    d. condemn

**3.** an **arid** discussion
a. informative    b. barren    c. heated    d. quiet

**4. confronted** my accuser
a. avoided    b. attacked    c. faced    d. ignored

**5.** an **instantaneous** decision
a. immediate    b. poor    c. delayed    d. wise

**6.** read the **synopsis**
a. report    b. summary    c. editorial    d. advertisement

**7.** a **gory** movie
a. foreign    b. new    c. bloody    d. funny

**8.** found him **dawdling**
a. loafing    b. working    c. fighting    d. napping

**9. scour** the countryside
a. visit    b. search    c. guard    d. invade

**10.** pay the **arrears**
a. back payments    b. prices    c. fines    d. taxes

**11.** a **deluge** of congratulations
a. shortage    b. trickle    c. flood    d. absence

**12.** played a **sluggish** game
a. new    b. slow    c. winning    d. brilliant

**13.** keep as a **memento**
a. reminder    b. safeguard    c. pet    d. ornament

**14.** the **onset** of the battle
a. conclusion    b. scene    c. beginning    d. noise

**15.** the **inevitable** result
a. sudden    b. unavoidable    c. regrettable    d. unexpected

**16.** a **parody** of justice
a. mockery    b. example    c. cause    d. fear

**17.** corrected the **misapprehension**
a. flavor    b. formula    c. examination    d. misunderstanding

**18. appended** her signature
a. forged    b. added    c. erased    d. examined

**19.** provided the necessary **data**
a. information    b. money    c. assistance    d. equipment

**20. restricted** his activities
a. limited    b. widened    c. guided    d. ended

**21.** a skilled **mimic**
a. athlete    b. politician    c. speaker    d. imitator

**22.** managed to **retrieve** the ball
a. inflate    b. recover    c. lose    d. puncture

**23.** met with **scant** success
a. much    b. little    c. popular    d. sudden

**24.** showed more **grit** than anyone else
a. judgment    b. fear    c. courage    d. restlessness

**25.** a **serene** mountain lake
a. peaceful    b. polluted    c. cold    d. large

---

**II. Antonyms**    *In each of the following groups, encircle the two words that are most nearly **opposite** in meaning.*

**26.**  a. clarity    b. trait    c. murkiness    d. sham

**27.**  a. clever    b. frigid    c. smug    d. hot

**28.**  a. affluence    b. diversity    c. strife    d. poverty

**29.**  a. wither    b. acquit    c. thrive    d. amble

**30.**  a. inhabitant    b. oaf    c. pacifist    d. warmonger

**31.**  a. rotund    b. compliant    c. boisterous    d. headstrong

**32.**  a. expend    b. pacify    c. occupy    d. vacate

**33.**  a. skillful    b. bumbling    c. optional    d. taut

**34.**  a. partisan    b. petty    c. sinister    d. impartial

**35.**  a. empower    b. conserve    c. squander    d. underscore

**36.**  a. verge    b. deter    c. idolize    d. detest

**37.**  a. maximum    b. giddy    c. celestial    d. minimum

**38.**  a. abstain    b. confiscate    c. indulge    d. enumerate

**39.**  a. strident    b. responsive    c. incalculable    d. mellow

**40.**  a. douse    b. relish    c. adhere    d. loathe

## III. Supplying Words in Context

*In each of the following sentences, write in the blank space the most appropriate word chosen from the list for that group.*

### Group A

| | | | |
|---|---|---|---|
| refute | immense | prevail | gainful |
| delude | vow | maze | debut |

41. The _____ distances between stars are measured in light-years.

42. You are just _____ yourself if you think you can do well in school without regular, systematic study.

43. Now that the two candidates have finished their long, hard campaigns, it is up to the voters to say which one will _____ .

44. Let us _____ to do the very best we can to carry out our duties honestly, efficiently, and humanely.

45. His arguments were so soundly based and so well presented that no one could _____ them.

### Group B

| | | | |
|---|---|---|---|
| keepsake | pantomime | misrepresent | unerring |
| sabotage | rendezvous | sleuth | eerie |

46. In the days of silent movies, actors and actresses had to express ideas and emotions by means of _____ .

47. We have learned by experience that she is so shrewd that her judgments of people are almost _____ .

48. I cannot believe that these repeated breakdowns of the machinery are no more than "accidents"; I suspect _____ !

49. My long-awaited _____ with Eileen turned out to be a terrible flop when she got sick and couldn't make it.

50. What a(n) _____ feeling it gave us to listen to ghost stories as we sat around the flickering campfire!

### Group C

| | | | |
|---|---|---|---|
| fray | epic | tally | subordinate |
| taskmaster | puncture | compact | allegiance |

51. The story of the men who first climbed to the top of Mount Everest is a(n) _____ of human courage and strength.

52. In big-city apartment houses, where space is very valuable, kitchens are likely to be extremely _____ .

**53.** I am grateful to my parents, who have always _____ their own interests and desires to the well-being of their children.

**54.** Coach Robinson is a strict _____ , who expects instant obedience and 100% effort from all his players.

**55.** Only a tiny _____ in the skin showed where the doctor had made the injection.

---

**IV. Words That Are Unfavorable**  *The words listed below are **unfavorable** or **negative**. Select the one that applies most suitably to each of the following short descriptive sentences or paragraphs. Write the word on the line provided.*

| | | | |
|---|---|---|---|
| **crotchety** | **bungle** | **self-seeking** | **cringe** |
| **libel** | **ingratitude** | **gloat** | **bigot** |
| **prevaricate** | **vandalism** | **hypocrite** | **uncouth** |

**56.** For no good reason, someone had tipped over the statue of Washington in the park and had tried to hammer it into pieces.  _____

**57.** No one can get along with him. You never know what is going to make him fly off the handle. He can get impossibly cranky fifty times a day.

_____

**58.** In that book, the author made a statement which he knew to be untrue and which was intended to ruin a political career.  _____

**59.** He is only interested in other people for what he can get out of them.

_____

**60.** She sat there with a big smile on her face, obviously enjoying the fact that I was in the most painful situation of my life.  _____

**61.** The mechanic did such a bad job of repairing our car that he actually caused us additional trouble and expense.  _____

**62.** What do you think of people who have strong prejudices against anyone who differs from them in race, religion, or social background?

_____

**63.** Some children are not thankful for all that their parents have done for them and are always demanding more.  _____

**64.** You can't depend on a word he says. He seems to tell lies for the sheer joy of lying.  _____

**65.** As my grandmother used to say, "anyone with manners that bad must have been raised in a stable."  _____

128

## V. Words That Are Favorable

*The words listed below are **favorable** or **positive**. Select the one that applies most suitably to each of the following short descriptive sentences or paragraphs. Write the word on the line provided.*

| sage | persevere | optimist | initiative |
|------|-----------|----------|------------|
| wholesome | disinterested | amiable | fidelity |
| discretion | acute | strapping | fluent |

**66.** Professor Hahn has had a wide range of experience and has thought deeply about the problems of life. He has much wisdom to give to his students. _____

**67.** The reason she is so attractive is that she gives the impression of radiant health, not only physically but also mentally and morally. _____

**68.** She takes a positive and upbeat attitude toward life. She believes that most problems can be solved and that things usually work out for the best. _____

**69.** Once he starts something, he keeps at it with all his energy. He won't let himself get discouraged, even when things go wrong. _____

**70.** He is a big, husky fellow, with the strength and the stamina of a professional athlete. _____

**71.** We admire her because she can get things started on her own, without being supported or guided by other people. _____

**72.** He is faithful to his family and friends, true to his religion, loyal to his community and his country. _____

**73.** When the judge hears a case, she has only one concern—to arrive at a just and fair decision. _____

**74.** He is a naturally friendly young man, who can get along pleasantly with almost anyone. _____

**75.** We greatly admire the sharpness of her mind. She sees right through to the heart of a problem without being misled by secondary matters. _____

## VI. Word Associations

*In each of the following, encircle the expression that best completes the meaning of the sentence or answers the question, with particular reference to the meaning of the word in **boldface type**.*

**76.** A study program might properly be called **intensive** if it
a. is a lot of fun
b. is open to everyone
c. calls for hours of hard work
d. will help you get a summer job

**77.** A basketball player who lacks **stamina** would be likely to
a. miss foul shots
b. tire quickly
c. argue with the referee
d. show a lack of team spirit

**78.** A school course dealing with **vocations** will help you
a. plan for a career
b. become a good dancer
c. become a "math shark"
d. develop your speaking ability

**79.** Which of the following might be a suitable nickname for a person who is **glum** most of the time?
a. "Deadeye Dick"
b. "Waltzing Matilda"
c. "Dapper Dan"
d. "Weeping Willie"

**80.** A crisis is said to be **global** if it applies to
a. only one nation
b. almost all the nations of the world
c. big business
d. transportation

**81.** For what purpose might you join a **queue**?
a. to make new friends
b. to see a hit movie
c. to speak at a school assembly
d. to enjoy a beautiful day

**82.** If you were **ravenous**, you might head for a
a. hospital
b. restaurant
c. library
d. skating rink

**83.** A person who is generally considered to be an **oracle** should be
a. kept in a closed room
b. put on a diet
c. listened to carefully
d. turned over to the police

**84.** A person who **reminisces** a great deal might be critcized for
a. living in the past
b. insulting other people
c. using foul language
d. borrowing money

**85.** You would seek **sanctuary** if you were
a. hungry
b. being pursued
c. in the dark
d. rich

**86.** If you receive news that is **disquieting**, you will probably be
a. delighted
b. serene
c. pleasantly surprised
d. upset

**87.** Which of the following might best be described by **saunter**?
a. a 50-yard run for a touchdown
b. a stroll in the park
c. a mad dash to catch a bus
d. a forced march

**88.** The word **martial** comes from the name of the Roman god Mars. We can guess from this that Mars was the god of
a. love
b. war
c. good health
d. farming

**89.** A person who is wearing **manacles** is probably a
a. prisoner
b. model
c. judge
d. teacher

**90.** If you are in a debating contest and you want to be **logical**, you should
a. smile a great deal
b. speak in a loud voice
c. make fun of your opponents
d. try to reason accurately

**91.** A **pessimist** is a person who
a. is sure everything will turn out for the worst
b. expects the best but is prepared for bad luck
c. refuses to worry about what the future may bring
d. depends on fortune-tellers for guidance

**92.** Which of the following would be a **chastening** experience?
a. winning a scholarship
b. going to a party
c. spending the day at the beach
d. doing poorly on this exam

**93.** A person who has carried out an **abduction** will probably
a. receive a prize
b. be arrested for kidnapping
c. get a ticket for illegal parking
d. go to the hospital

**94.** Which of the following would have **facets?**
a. a planet
b. an umbrella
c. a diamond
d. a chair

**95.** For performing a **valiant** deed, a soldier would probably be
a. transferred
b. given a medal
c. called a coward
d. given a new uniform

**96.** A ballplayer would be most likely to receive an **ovation** for
a. winning a game with a home run
b. losing a game by striking out
c. arguing with the umpire
d. not playing because of an injury

**97.** A student who is lost in a **reverie**
a. has taken a wrong turn
b. has a toothache
c. is daydreaming
d. is well prepared for final exams

**98.** A habit that is deeply **ingrained** is
a. a bad one
b. hard to change
c. easy to get rid of
d. of no great importance

**99.** Which of the following is typical of **contemporary** life?
a. hoopskirts and sun bonnets
b. TV and computers
c. colonies in outer space
d. log cabins

**100.** You will **affirm** your mastery of the words taught in this book if you
a. spell them incorrectly
b. forget what they mean
c. never use them in class
d. score 100% on this Final Test

# Building with Prefixes

## Units 1–3

**de**—down; away from; completely; not

This prefix appears in **denounce** (page 10), **depict** (page 15), and **designate** (page 20). Other words in which this prefix appears are listed below.

| | | | |
|---|---|---|---|
| **debunk** | **default** | **demerit** | **desperate** |
| **decapitate** | **defraud** | **depression** | **devolve** |

*From the list of words above, choose the one that corresponds to each of the brief definitions below. Write the word in the space at the right of the definition, and then in the illustrative phrase below it.*

**1.** to cheat, take away from or deprive of by deceit or trickery       _____

_____ of her rightful inheritance

**2.** driven to take any risk; hopeless; extreme       _____

a _____ measure

**3.** a mark against, usually involving the loss of some privilege or right; a fault, defect       _____

behavior that earned him a _____

**4.** to cut off the head, behead       _____

_____ a fish before cooking it

**5.** to expose the falseness of unsound or exaggerated claims       _____

_____ a time-honored legend

**6.** to fail to perform a task or fulfill an obligation; the failure to do something required by law or duty       _____

won by _____

**7.** to pass on (a duty, task, or the like) to someone else; to be passed on to, be conferred on       _____

when his powers _____ on his successor

**8.** an area that is sunk below its surroundings; a period of severe economic decline; a mood of dejection or sadness       _____

during the Great _____ of the 1930's

*From the list of words on page 131, choose the one that best completes each of the following sentences. Write the word in the space provided.*

**1.** Posing as investment counselors, the pair of wily swindlers managed to

_____ the elderly couple of most of their savings.

**2.** Over the years, historians have _____ many of the famous stories associated with George Washington because they have no basis in fact.

**3.** When the debtor failed to repay the loan, the bank was forced to declare

him in _____ .

**4.** On the whole, I think that the new program's good points far outnumber its

_____ .

**5.** The firefighters made one last, _____ attempt to save the lives of the people still trapped in the burning building.

**6.** When my boss became ill, many of the duties and responsibilities of his

job suddenly _____ on me.

**7.** Scores of those condemned to death by the French revolutionary tribunals

were _____ by the guillotine.

**8.** After we had lost the championship game, we returned to the locker room

in a profound state of _____ .

# Units 4–6

**re**—back; again

This prefix appears in **repent** (page 32), **revocation** (page 32), **refute** (page 37), **remorse** (page 37), and **reimburse** (page 42). Other words in which this prefix appears are listed below.

| | | | |
|---|---|---|---|
| **rebuke** | **refrain** | **renege** | **retract** |
| **redeem** | **relic** | **restraint** | **revive** |

*From the list of words above, choose the one that corresponds to each of the brief definitions below. Write the word in the space at the right of the definition, and then in the illustrative phrase below it.*

**1.** to go back on a promise                                    _____

_____ on the deal

**2.** to hold oneself back; a repeated verse, chorus _____

_____ from overeating

**3.** to take back something that has been said,
offered, or published _____

demanded that the newspaper _____ the story

**4.** to buy back; to make up for; to fulfill a pledge _____

_____ the loan

**5.** to scold, express sharp disapproval; a scolding _____

_____ the children for misbehaving

**6.** a device that restricts or confines; control over the
expression of one's feelings or behavior _____

placed _____ on the violent prisoner

**7.** something that has survived the passage of time _____

searched for Indian _____

**8.** to give new life to; to restore _____

_____ their dampened spirits

---

*From the list of words on page 132, choose the one that
best completes each of the following sentences. Write
the word in the space provided.*

**1.** The fans were asked to _____ from rushing onto the court
until the basketball game was officially over.

**2.** When she _____ on her promise, we felt that we could no
longer trust her to keep her word.

**3.** The rescue squad worked frantically to _____ the boy who
had been overcome by smoke.

**4.** The recruit's failure to salute earned him a stern _____ from
the sergeant.

**5.** It took remarkable _____ on the part of the speaker not to
respond to the taunts of the hecklers.

**6.** Dressed in their old campaign uniforms, the aging veterans looked like

_____ of a bygone age.

**7.** "If you do not immediately _____ those outrageous
allegations," declared the lawyer, "my client will sue for libel."

**8.** The rookie's brilliant play in the final game of the series more than

_____ the crucial error he had made in the opener.

# Units 7–9

**il, im, in, ir**—in; not

This prefix appears in **illicit** (page 54), **immobile** (page 59), **innovation** (page 59), and **impact** (page 64). Some other words in which this prefix appears are listed below.

| | | | |
|---|---|---|---|
| **illuminate** | **impressionable** | **inauguration** | **invigorate** |
| **implant** | **impudent** | **intolerable** | **irrational** |

*From the list of words above, choose the one that corresponds to each of the brief definitions below. Write the word in the space at the right of the definition, and then in the illustrative phrase below it.*

**1.** not to be endured or suffered; excessive   _____

an _____ burden

**2.** a formal beginning or introduction   _____

the _____ of a new era

**3.** contrary to reason; insane   _____

_____ fears

**4.** to light up, bring light to   _____

searchlights that _____ the night sky

**5.** rude, disrespectful, insolent, shameless   _____

a(n) _____ remark

**6.** to give energy or strength to, fill with vitality   _____

was _____ by the fresh air

**7.** to set in firmly, instill; to fix deeply   _____

_____ high ideals in the children's minds

**8.** easily influenced; capable of being molded or imprinted   _____

as _____ as soft clay

*From the list of words above, choose the one that best completes each of the following sentences. Write the word in the space provided.*

**1.** When the pain in his chest became _____ , the wounded soldier cried out in anguish for some relief.

**2.** As the emperor's behavior grew more and more _____ , his advisors began to suspect that he was losing his reason.

**3.** Although his lengthy explanation was supposed to _____ the problem, it left me completely in the dark.

**4.** A healthy diet and regular exercise _____ the body.

**5.** "I am beginning to lose patience with that _____ smart aleck," my boss complained, "and his endless back talk."

**6.** The _____ of a new administration is often marked by a "honeymoon" between the President and Congress.

**7.** Since young children are extremely _____ , we must be careful to shield them from things that are frightening.

**8.** Once a prejudice is deeply _____ , it is very difficult to uproot it.

---

# Units 10–12

**co, col, com, con, cor**—with, together

This prefix appears in **consequence** (page 77), **compact** (page 87), and **confer** (page 87). Some other words in which this prefix appears are listed below.

| | | | |
|---|---|---|---|
| **coincidence** | **colleague** | **compute** | **confide** |
| **collaborate** | **composure** | **concurrent** | **correspond** |

---

*From the list of words above, choose the one that corresponds to each of the brief definitions below. Write the word in the space at the right of the definition, and then in the illustrative phrase below it.*

**1.** occurring at the same time; agreeing; coming together _____

    sentenced to _____ prison terms

**2.** the chance occurrence of two things at the same time or place _____

    met by _____

**3.** to determine by arithmetic, reckon _____

    used a calculator to _____ the answer

**4.** to exchange letters; to be in agreement _____

    _____ by mail

**5.** calmness of mind, bearing, or appearance; self-control

could not ruffle his _____

**6.** to work with others; to aid or assist an enemy of one's country

_____ on the science project

**7.** to tell something as a secret; to entrust a secret

_____ in a friend

**8.** a fellow worker, associate

honored by her _____

---

*From the list of words on page 135, choose the one that best completes each of the following sentences. Write the word in the space provided.*

**1.** The composer George Gershwin often _____ with his brother Ira in writing some of America's best-loved songs.

**2.** The gossip columnist's success stemmed from her amazing ability to get celebrities to _____ in her.

**3.** Sherlock Holmes was often assisted in his investigations by his trusted friend and _____ , Dr. Watson.

**4.** The abacus is still widely used in China to _____ sums.

**5.** The culprits rehearsed their alibi until their stories _____ in each and every detail.

**6.** For a rookie making his first World Series appearance, the pitcher showed remarkable _____ and maturity on the mound.

**7.** Powers exercised at one and the same time by the states and the Federal government—for example, the power to tax—are said to be

_____ .

**8.** By some strange _____ , both Thomas Jefferson and John Adams died on exactly the same day, July 4, 1826.

# Units 13–15

**pre**—before

This prefix appears in **precaution** (page 111). Other words in which this prefix appears are listed below.

**prearrange**    **prefer**    **preliminary**    **preoccupy**
**precise**    **prehistoric**    **premature**    **preside**

*From the list of words above, choose the one that corresponds to each of the brief definitions below. Write the word in the space at the right of the definition, and then in the illustrative phrase below it.*

**1.** to absorb one's attention completely or at the expense of other things

_____ with her studies     _____

**2.** belonging to the period before written history

the bones of _____ animals     _____

**3.** very definite or clear, exact; very careful; strict

left _____ instructions     _____

**4.** coming before the main business or action; introductory; something that comes before the main event, a "curtain-raiser"

lost the _____ bout     _____

**5.** to arrange ahead of time

_____ a schedule     _____

**6.** to like better, choose over something else; to put forward, press

_____ English to math     _____

**7.** to be head of; to have authority over, oversee

_____ at the board meeting     _____

**8.** unexpectedly early in development; coming too soon

a _____ birth     _____

*From the list of words on page 137, choose the one that best completes each of the following sentences. Write the word in the space provided.*

1. The police _____ charges against the driver of one of the vehicles involved in the accident.

2. Cave paintings and artifacts found in the Southwest are the only traces remaining of certain _____ American Indian cultures.

3. The Vice President _____ over the Senate.

4. They claimed that their meeting was accidental and unplanned, but in fact they had _____ it.

5. Although polls showed an upset in the making, analysts cautioned that it would be _____ to declare the underdog the winner.

6. The thieves were so _____ with dividing up the loot that they failed to notice that the police had surrounded their hideout.

7. The directions for assembling the bike were so _____ that we had no difficulty at all in putting it together.

8. A _____ hearing was held to determine whether there was sufficient evidence to try the accused.

# Index

The following tabulation lists all the basic words taught in the various units of this workbook, as well as those introduced in the *Vocabulary of Vocabulary* and *Building with Prefixes* sections. The number after each item indicates the page on which it is introduced, but the word may also appear in exercises on later pages.

ingratitude, 31
inhabitant, 36
initiative, 77
innovation, 59
instantaneous, 11
intensive, 87
intimidate, 64
intolerable, 134
invigorate, 134
irk, 11
irrational, 134

jovial, 59

keepsake, 31

lag, 101
leeway, 41
libel, 11
liberate, 64
limber, 42
literal, 4
logical, 64

manacle, 59
maneuver, 87
mangle, 101
manipulate, 15
martial, 59
maximum, 16
maze, 42
memento, 77
memorandum, 54
meteoric, 82
mimic, 16
minimum, 59
misapprehension, 101
misgiving, 11
misrepresent, 64
mortal, 31
motivate, 20

nimble, 59
nonconformist, 77
null and void, 77
numb, 36

oaf, 11
onset, 60
optimist, 101
optional, 64
oracle, 42
outright, 64
ovation, 31

pacifist, 20
pacify, 37
panorama, 77
pantomime, 111
parody, 83
partisan, 42
partition, 60
pathetic, 54
perishable, 60
persevere, 55
pessimist, 111
petty, 31
plight, 31
posterity, 78
prearrange, 137
precaution, 111
precise, 137
prefer, 137
prefix, 3
prehistoric, 137
preliminary, 137
premature, 137
preoccupy, 137
preside, 137
prevail, 83
prevaricate, 55
prosecute, 111
prowl, 102
pry, 78
puncture, 112

quash, 55
queue, 20

ravenous, 37
rebuke, 132
recede, 11
redeem, 132
refrain, 132
refurbish, 78
refute, 37
reimburse, 42
relic, 132
relish, 55
reminisce, 55
remorse, 37
rend, 83
rendezvous, 64
renege, 132
repast, 11
repent, 32
replenish, 83
replica, 106
resourceful, 78
responsive, 106

restraint, 132
restrict, 20
retaliate, 112
retract, 132
retrieve, 60
reverie, 32
revive, 132
revocation, 32
rigorous, 78
root, 3
rotund, 65
ruffle, 16
rummage, 83

sabotage, 87
sage, 21
sanctuary, 107
saunter, 65
scan, 32
scant, 88
scour, 55
self-seeking, 107
serene, 16
setback, 37
sham, 112
sheepish, 16
sinister, 60
skimp, 83
slake, 21
sleuth, 83
sluggish, 65
smug, 37
stamina, 16
stealthy, 88
strand, 32
strapping, 88
strident, 88
strife, 32
stupefy, 102
submissive, 107
subordinate, 65
subsequent, 78
suffix, 3
sulky, 102
supplement, 102
surge, 102
synonym, 1
synopsis, 37

tally, 107
tarry, 37
taskmaster, 107
taut, 60
terrain, 21
thrive, 88

tint, 65
titanic, 88
topple, 32
trait, 102
transform, 107

uncouth, 112
underscore, 112
unerring, 78
unscrupulous, 102
upheaval, 107

vacate, 42
vagabond, 42
valiant, 88
vandalism, 83
variable, 65
verge, 65
vocation, 21
vow, 21

waylay, 21
wholesome, 112
wistful, 112
wither, 21
writhe, 55